Fundamentals of Financial Services

Edition 4, May 2019

This learning manual covers examinations from
1 August 2019 to 31 July 2021

APPROVED WORKBOOK

FUNDAMENTALS OF FINANCIAL SERVICES

Welcome to the Chartered Institute for Securities & Investment's Fundamentals of Financial Services study material.

This learning workbook has been written to prepare you for the Chartered Institute for Securities & Investment's examination.

PUBLISHED BY:
Chartered Institute for Securities & Investment
© Chartered Institute for Securities & Investment 2019
20 Fenchurch Street
London
EC3M 3BY
Tel: +44 20 7645 0600
Fax: +44 20 7645 0601

Written by Martin Mitchell FCSI
Reviewers
Natasha Manrai
Simon Culhane, Chartered FCSI

A Learning Map, which contains the full syllabus, appears at the end of this workbook. The syllabus can also be viewed on the Institute's website at cisi.org and is also available by contacting Customer Support on +44 20 7645 0777. Please note that the exam is based on the syllabus.

Candidates are reminded to check the Candidate Update area of the Institute's website (cisi.org/candidateupdate) on a regular basis for updates that could affect their exam as a result of industry change.

The questions contained in this workbook are designed as an aid to revision of different areas of the syllabus and to help you consolidate your learning chapter by chapter. They should not be seen as a 'mock' exam or necessarily indicative of the level of the questions in the corresponding exam.

Workbook version: 4.1 (May 2019)

FOREWORD

Learning with the CISI

You are now studying for an exam that will introduce you to the Fundamentals of Financial Services. This workbook and the accompanying elearning product is designed to provide you with interesting information and to enable you to know more about and understand how this important industry functions.

You may not have heard of the CISI, but over 40,000 individuals are members, the vast majority of whom work in the profession. We hope that this exam will help you to build awareness of career opportunities and personal financial knowledge. So whether you are in work or education, you will find this useful.

When you register for the exam, you will be able to access a wide range of resources on our website (cisi.org), which will not only help with your studies, but help to broaden awareness of all aspects of the investment and banking world.

We hope that this thorough grounding in the essentials will encourage you to consider financial services as a career option.

This workbook and elearning product are updated regularly, so please check to ensure you have the correct version for your exam. As well as using industry specialists to update and review the material, we also use students and tutors to ensure that the material is relevant to your needs and level of experience.

We really hope that you enjoy your studies with the CISI and that you find the learning experience a stimulating one.

CONTENTS

It is estimated that this workbook will require approximately 60 hours of study time.

Before you open Chapter 1

It's free

We love a book! ...but don't forget you have been sent a link to an ebook, which gives you a range of tools to help you study for this qualification

Depending on the individual subject being studied and your device, your ebook may include features such as:

Watch video clips related to your syllabus

Read aloud function*

Adjustable text size allows you to read comfortably on any device*

Pop-up definitions

Highlight, bookmark and make annotations digitally*

Images, tables and animated graphs

Links to relevant websites

End of chapter questions and interactive multiple choice questions

* These features are device dependent. Please consult your manufacturers guidelines for compatibility

Ethics and Integrity in Financial Services

This syllabus area will provide approximately 1 of the 30 examination questions

Ethics and Integrity in Financial Services

1. Introduction

Learning Objective 1.1.1

Know the key principles of ethical behaviour in financial services

What does behaving ethically mean to you? Do you think you know? Of course you do! Who doesn't? Everyone knows. It is about being honest, fair and doing things properly.

Words frequently used alongside, or sometimes instead of ethics include; values, integrity and morals.

Most of us face ethical choices on a regular basis, and doing the right thing is usually obvious, particularly in our personal lives. For

example, you are not likely to steal your friend's mobile phone. But what would you do if you found a mobile phone on the bus, particularly a top-of-the-range model that you have been saving towards buying for yourself?

Might you be tempted to keep it?

Perhaps, but you know that it is not yours and it is worth at least £500, so the thought of keeping it should make you feel uncomfortable.

Accordingly, you decide that you will hand it to the driver, whom you trust to hand it to the bus company's lost property office. So doing the right thing – acting ethically – would appear straightforward.

So, why are there so many reported business situations in which seemingly rational people are said to have behaved unethically?

- Is it because they chose to do so?
- Is it because they consider that there are some situations where ethics apply and others where they do not?
- Is it because they did not think that their behaviour was unethical?
- Or, perhaps it was just that they thought they could get away with it?

Could it be that it involves a combination of all of these thoughts and actions, as well as some more perhaps?

There is also the question of why ethical behaviour has become such an issue, particularly in financial services. If ethics are as important as people are now saying, then surely they have always been important?

The answer to that is a resounding 'yes'. Ethical behaviour has always been important. The collective failure of those working in the financial services sector to keep the importance of ethical behaviour in the forefront of their minds and actions was a major contributor to the huge loss of trust suffered by the sector and, unfortunately, trust is much easier to lose than it is to restore. As the Governor of the **Bank of England** said, '*Trust arrives on foot, but leaves in a Ferrari*'.

2.   **Ethics in Practice**

This might be simply rephrased as 'doing the right thing'. The key point about ethical decision-making is that you make the choice about the action that you take. Ethics and regulation, or the law, are not one and the same thing. You may act unethically without breaking the law; your actions may be unpleasant or antisocial but not illegal. However, if you break the law, your actions will be both unethical and illegal.

One of the observations sometimes made about ethics is that the benefit of ignoring ethical standards and behaviour far outweighs the benefit of adhering to them, both from an individual and also from a corporate perspective.

In other words, an action taken simply because it seems to be in the best interests of the doer (you) makes obvious sense. In the earlier example of finding the mobile phone on the bus, keeping the phone is to your advantage. You have something that you want and you have not actively stolen it; you've simply found it. You do not know the owner (the person who lost it), so you do not have a personal connection which might influence your behaviour.

However, what this argument ignores is that, while a policy of acting in your own interests may seem to make sense and be sustainable for a short period, in our society the inevitable outcome is likely to be at least social and at worst criminal sanctions.

In addition, the fact is that either of these outcomes, whether social or legal sanction, is likely to overturn whatever economic justification there appeared to be for the unethical behaviour. In other words, any apparent short-term advantage is likely to be a small fraction of the inevitable long-term damage.

So what might you do when faced with a situation where doing the right thing may not be immediately obvious? There is one simple question, with four key principles embedded within it, that you should ask yourself:

> *Is what I am about to do, or are the actions that I am about to take,* **open**, **honest**, **transparent** *and* **fair**?

To test this, let's go back to the mobile phone example. Instead of handing in the phone to the driver, you decide that you will keep it. How would your actions in keeping a valuable phone, which you had found, not stolen, measure up to the test?

- Was your action **open**? Did you ask anyone on the bus if they had dropped their phone, or look around to see if anyone was searching for it? Did you try and find out who the phone belonged to and return it? If not, your action cannot be said to be open.
- Was your action **honest**? This should be simple. You found the phone. It does not belong to you; it belongs to someone else and the fact that you do not know whom is irrelevant. Keeping it for yourself cannot be considered honest.
- Was your action **transparent**? This depends on your reaction to your friends admiring your new phone. If you are reluctant to say how you came to have the phone your actions are not transparent.
- Was your action **fair**? How can you claim that keeping something that does not belong to you is fair? You have deprived the rightful owner of their possession. There is a mechanism for returning lost property and you haven't used it.

What seemed like a good idea at the time should now be coming back to haunt you!

3. Ethics in Financial Services

As we mentioned at the beginning of this chapter, the integrity of people and practices in financial services has been undermined by a number of recent scandals, one example of which has been the rigging of LIBOR (the London Interbank Offered Rate) and other interest rate setting mechanisms around the world.

Banks are supposed to submit the actual interest rates they are paying, or would expect to pay, for borrowing from other banks so that benchmark **interest** rates (such as the LIBOR rate) can be set. Having a set interest rate is necessary as it serves as a benchmark for setting the price of government and corporate **bonds**, **mortgages**, student **loans**, credit cards and other financial products (which will be covered later in this workbook).

However, it was discovered that some traders working at banks, such as Barclays, Lloyds, UBS, Deutsche Bank, JPMorgan Chase, Bank of America and HSBC, had been falsely inflating or deflating interest rates in order to profit from **trades**, or to give the impression they were more creditworthy than they actually were. While this benefited banks and individual traders involved in the scandal, benchmark interest rates are used to calculate financial products for people trying to obtain a mortgage or take out a student loan, and so had significant negative effects on consumers and financial **markets** around the world. This eventually resulted in billions of dollars of fines for the banks involved as well as jail sentences for some of the guilty individuals.

The outcome of this approach was that the interests of the customer became secondary to the interest of the banks and individual traders, which is the complete reverse of what the relationship should be. The banks and those individuals involved in the scandal were not behaving in a way that was **open**, **honest**, **transparent** or **fair**.

Another area of financial services which is particularly open to the risk of unethical behaviour is sales. The examples below discuss the ethics of selling in financial services in a little more depth.

⚙ Example

A company has designed an acceptable product and is trying to establish how best to sell it in the face of competition. The company decides that the best means of doing this is to pay a sales commission for each product sold.

The sales force is remunerated on the basis of performance. The more they sell, the more they earn.

It can be argued that there is nothing wrong with such a structure, which simply reflects an established method of doing business around the world and applies to almost any large or even not so large item.

But there are fundamental differences in the financial services sector which particularly may affect the relationship between the salesperson and the customer.

For example, if you buy a car, you can see it, you can try it out and you will discover very quickly whether it performs in the manner advertised and which you expect. You will also be provided, in the case of a new car, with a warranty from the manufacturer. You can thus make your decision to buy with considerable confidence, despite knowing that the reward system in the motor industry means that the salesperson will almost certainly receive a **commission** as a result of your purchase.

Contrast this with an imaginary financial product:

⚙ Example

You, the customer, wish to make financial provision for the future, either by buying a product for a lump sum, or via a stream of payments over a period. You see an advertisement for a financial product which seems attractive: it promises a return of 5% per annum, compared with the 2% per annum which your savings will receive in the bank.

You contact the company, which has a well-known name, although you have had no previous dealings with them. A salesperson comes to see you and explains the product in general terms, focusing particularly on the return offered by the product. They explain to you the mechanism by which the company improves the return to you, over and above what you would receive from your bank. You are not financially aware and do not really understand everything the salesperson is saying.

You are now entering the area where, particularly in the financial services sector, the greatest opportunity arises for the salesperson either to display adherence to ethical values and behaviours or to ignore them. The customer who buys a financial product is buying something whose performance is likely to be determined over a period of time. The ethical salesperson will take you through the structure of the product offered in such a manner that you may be reasonably sure that you understand what it is and from whom you are buying. They will explain the risk factors which determine the rate of **return** that is offered, and tell you whether that is an actual rate or an anticipated rate which is dependent upon certain other things happening, over which the product originator may have no control. They will also tell you what they are being paid if you buy the product.

In other words, the ethical salesperson will give you all the facts that you need to make an informed decision as to whether you wish to invest. They will be **open, honest, transparent** and **fair**.

Conversely, an unethical salesperson may seek to convince you with phrases such as 'no-one else has asked me about that', or 'don't worry, I wouldn't sell a product that I didn't have confidence in', or 'no, I don't understand it either, but we have rocket scientists to design these things'. Or they may suggest that this is a limited opportunity and you need to decide now if you wish to take advantage of it.

The salesperson might reassure and convince you with bland words that actually convey nothing, and you will be encouraged to make a decision without sufficient facts. Consider whether they are being **open, honest, transparent** and **fair**? Fairly obviously not.

Is the salesperson displaying ethical values, qualities and behaviours?

Again, it is clear that they are not.

Exercise 1

Consider what you have just read and think how you could apply the four principles to:

- *a situation at home or in your private life*
- *a situation at work*
- *a situation reported in the media.*

You should now be able to rationalise what is the right and ethical thing to do by using the principles.

Exercise 2

The four key principles and tests to assess whether or not behaviour is ethical revolve around whether the action taken was open, honest, transparent and which of the following?

a. *Fair*
b. *Balanced*
c. *Legal*
d. *Harmless*

⚙ Answers to Chapter Exercises

Exercise 2 – Ethical Behaviour

1. A (chapter 1, section 3).

2. The four ethical principles are to assess whether the behaviour was open, honest, transparent and fair.

Saving and Borrowing

This syllabus area will provide approximately 4 of the 30 examination questions

Saving and Borrowing

1. Introduction

Learning Objective 2.1.1

Know how the financial services sector can be viewed as linking those with surplus money (savers) and those with a need for money (borrowers) in the following ways: via banks (deposits, loans); via equities (ownership stake); via bonds (IOUs)

Let's not fool ourselves. The financial services sector looks pretty complicated to most of us. Why is this? Well, it's primarily because of the technical jargon that is used to explain things: bonds, shares, **funds**, interest rates and **inflation** rates are just some of the many examples. This workbook will unravel most of the complexity and you will emerge with sufficient understanding to deal confidently with

financial matters. You will have the ability to ask relevant and sensible questions and be able to properly comprehend the answers.

This could help you in a variety of ways. Perhaps a job in finance is right for you. Perhaps you simply need to be able to manage your own, or your family's, financial affairs better. Hopefully, this course of study will help you do either one, or both!

To start with, let's try to portray the world of finance as simply as we can. Let's think of it as the link between two groups – we will call one of them the 'savers' and the other the 'borrowers'. The savers are fortunate – they have more money than they need right now – so they want to do something with their surplus money that will hopefully see it grow.

These savers could be individuals, companies or governments, and some of them have a lot more surplus money than others. The financial services world tends to refer to individuals who have substantial amounts of surplus money as 'high net worth individuals' (HNWIs). Some companies also have a lot of spare cash, for example Apple had around $26 billion in its bank accounts at the end of 2018.

Like savers, the borrowers can also be individuals, companies and governments.

An example of a borrower might be a small **start-up** idea, such as CareerComic, as detailed below.

⚙ Example

Two young college graduates have a great idea. They think that other college graduates and schoolkids would love to have access to a database of available careers that is portrayed in a fun, simple and understandable way. They want to pull together a comic strip of a day in the life of each career – CareerComic.

They have talked to people about their plans for CareerComic and they have potentially found someone – an investor – who will provide them with some money to produce a high-quality example of how the comic will look. In return for their investment, the investor will be given a 50% share of the business – they are hoping the business might grow and be worth a lot of money one day.

It is the financial markets that provide the link between savers and borrowers. The link between the two is provided in three main ways – by the banks, by **equity** and by bonds – each of which is explained in the following paragraphs.

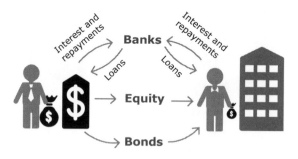

1.1 The Role of Banks

Traditionally, banks have provided a convenient link between savers and borrowers, making a profit on the difference between what they pay savers and what they charge borrowers.

The savers **deposit** their surplus money at the bank, for which the bank is willing to pay interest – say, 5% per annum. The bank will then lend the deposited money on to borrowers, perhaps charging them 8% per annum interest on the loans. So, if a bank attracted a combined £100 million in deposits, it would need to pay £5 million interest for the year (5% x £100 million). If the bank managed to lend the £100 million, it would receive £8 million interest for the year (8% x £100 million). By receiving interest of £8 million and paying interest of only £5 million, the bank is generating a £3 million surplus. This is not profit, but a surplus from which its various costs need to be paid, such as staff wages, office rental payments and taxes. What is left after deducting these costs is profit.

Banks

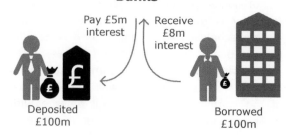

1.2 Equity

For businesses looking to raise money, an alternative to borrowing from banks is for the business to sell equity. Equity is alternatively referred to as shares or stock and it represents ownership. The holders of the equity in a company own that company. So, if a business is set up as a company, it can raise money by selling shares. This is exactly what happened in the earlier CareerComic example – finance was raised by selling an equity stake in the business.

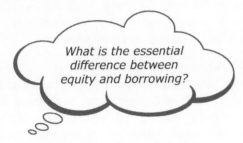

What is the essential difference between equity and borrowing?

So, why might equity be preferred as a source of finance to borrowing? There are a number of differences between the two that will need to be considered and which will be explored a little later in the chapter with a further look at CareerComic. For the moment, perhaps the key differences are that interest needs to be paid on borrowing, and the money borrowed has to be repaid. There is no interest paid on equity and equity does not need to be repaid.

It is not only start-ups that raise money by selling equity – big companies occasionally sell large quantities of equity in **initial public offerings** (**IPOs**). A good example is the massive IPO of Chinese e-commerce giant Alibaba in September 2014.

⚙ Example

The Alibaba IPO

*Alibaba sold 368 million shares at $68 per share in September 2014, raising just over $25 billion in total ($8 billion of which was **capital** for the company), and allowing some earlier investors to sell their shares at a substantial profit. The most significant earlier investor was Yahoo, which sold shares in the IPO for a total of $10.2 billion.*

However, if these early investors had held onto their shares, then by February 2019, they would have more than doubled their investments as the shares had increased by $100 to $168.

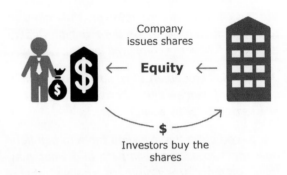

Company issues shares

Equity

Investors buy the shares

1.3 Bonds

The third major way that savers and borrowers are linked in the financial markets is where the borrowers issue IOUs (IOU = 'I owe you'), typically called bonds. These IOUs are issued directly to the investors, missing out the banks. Like a loan from a bank, borrowing money by issuing bonds is another form of debt on which the borrower will pay interest and which needs to be repaid.

If a borrower wants to raise £100 million, it could subdivide the amount into one million IOUs, each representing £100 – these are called bonds. The borrower might agree to pay the holders of the bonds their £100 back in ten years, and until that point agree to pay them a rate of interest each year. In this example, we are assuming the company pays interest to the lender of 7% each year.

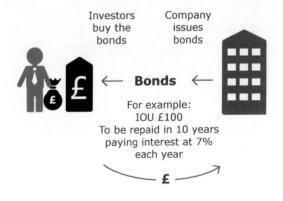

Investors buy the bonds

Company issues bonds

Bonds

For example:
IOU £100
To be repaid in 10 years
paying interest at 7%
each year

Exercise 1 – Financing Choices

Remember CareerComic is the idea of two young college graduates. They think that other college graduates and schoolchildren would love to have access to a database of available careers in the form of a comic strip of a day in the life of each career. However, they need to raise some finance to produce a high-quality example of how the comic will look.

Businesses like CareerComic have two potential sources of finance – either borrowing the money or raising equity by selling shares.

Try to complete the following table to highlight how the two sources compare and what may have driven CareerComic to choose equity. Once you have completed the table, please compare your answers with the completed table in the appendix to the chapter.

Consideration	Borrowing or Equity?
Which one is more expensive (in terms of annual cash costs)?	?
Which one is likely to need to be repaid earlier?	?
Which one is more likely to be available for a start-up company?	?
Which one is likely to be the more risky for the finance provider?	?
Which one is likely to have the largest potential 'upside' for the finance provider?	?

Based on the above, can you understand why CareerComic chose to raise finance through equity?

2. Who are the Savers and Borrowers?

Learning Objective 2.1.2
Know that borrowers include companies and governments and that governments issue bonds rather than equities

We have already seen that many savers are individuals or firms with surplus money that they do not need right now. They will invest this money instead, perhaps by depositing it in a bank, or by buying bonds or equities.

The borrowers we have encountered so far are companies that are looking for finance either to start up (like CareerComic) or to grow from an already established base (like Alibaba). However, it is not only companies that borrow. We know that many individuals do not have surplus money, and instead have a shortage of money, particularly when it comes to financing high-cost items such as household items (washing machines, televisions and fridges) or a house itself. Clearly, such individuals can be borrowers when they take out loans to make such purchases. Loans to buy homes are known as mortgages.

As will be explored in chapter 3 of this workbook, there are different ways for individuals to borrow money. Sometimes the money is borrowed for a particular purpose, such as a mortgage loan to buy somewhere to live, or a car loan. On other occasions, money can be borrowed for a consumer item such as a widescreen TV or a washing machine. These are often simply described as **personal loans**. Furthermore, some forms of borrowing may need to be repaid earlier and some much later.

A good example is the bank **overdraft**, which is a form of loan on which the bank can demand repayment immediately. By contrast, a typical mortgage may not be totally repaid for 25 or 30 years.

One important group of borrowers that we have not yet encountered is governments. Many governments collect substantial sums of money each year by imposing taxes on their residents to spend on a variety of items, including roads, hospitals, defence, education and the wages of government staff.

In some cases, government expenditure exceeds government revenue. The difference needs to be financed in some way and it is generally borrowed.

However, government borrowing tends not to come from banks but from individuals and firms in the form of regular issues of bonds. Indeed, in 2016, the UK had outstanding bonds that added up to more than £1.5 trillion – that's one and a half thousand, billion pounds – and the US had more than $20 trillion! These amounts are known as the country's **national debt**.

Not all governments are borrowers. In places such as Norway, some Gulf States and Singapore, the government generates a surplus that puts it in the position of being a saver rather than a borrower.

In Norway and the Gulf, this is often due to an abundance of natural resources, particularly oil and gas. In Singapore, it is essentially due to a very successful economy and a government that is careful about how it spends its revenues.

3. Risk and Reward

Learning Objective 2.1.3

Know the relationship between the level of risk and the prospect of reward

We have established that there are a variety of possible ways that savers can invest their surplus money, particularly by depositing the money at a bank, or by buying equities or bonds. So what would make them choose one investment over another?

Have a look at the example below to discover a little more.

⚙ Example

Sophie has some money she wants to invest. She wants to be reasonably confident that she will be able to get all of her money back in two or three years' time, when she hopes to use the money as a deposit for the purchase of her first home. She has narrowed down two possibilities: an instant access bank deposit account that will pay 5% per annum, and a two-year bond issued by a company that will pay 7% per annum. Which one should she go for?

The answer is that it depends on what Sophie is looking for in terms of flexibility and how much risk she is willing to take with her money.

On the face of it, the two-year bond is better in that it pays interest that is 2% higher. However, the bond may be risky – it might be issued by a small company that may not have the cash to repay it in two years' time. The deposit account is instant access, so that if Sophie were to need her money earlier than planned, she could access it.

Therefore, it is Sophie's preference – to take possibly greater risk for greater reward, or to take less risk and accept a lower reward and/ or immediate access – which will ultimately determine which investment is right for her.

As the above example illustrates, making the right investment choice is not always straightforward. In fact, there is always a direct link between the risk the investor is willing to take and the potential reward that the investor might realise from the investment. It's the financial equivalent of the fitness industry saying 'no pain, no gain'. In investment terms, the less likely it is that the investor will lose money, the less spectacular the potential level of return the investor can hope for. Risk and reward run hand in hand.

Higher Reward

Increasing Risk

Bonds issued in US dollars by a country with a stuttering economy and unstable government.	?
Roulette wheel at a casino	?

More risky and less risky investments are sometimes straightforward to identify. If you were to buy shares in an established company like Microsoft® or Apple, there would generally be somewhat less risk, in the longer term, than if you were to invest in a loss-making, early-stage company. Similarly, investing your surplus money by putting it into an established bank's deposit account is likely to be significantly less risky than investing it by lending to a friend.

Try the following exercise to see if you can identify the riskier and, potentially, more rewarding investments:

Exercise 2 – Risk and Reward

Put the following investments in order, from the most risky (and potentially rewarding) to the least risky (and safer). The suggested answer can be found at the end of the chapter.

Investments	Risk ranking (where 1 is the highest risk and 6 the lowest risk)
US government bonds	?
Equities issued by a start-up company	?
Equities issued by a large, well-established company	?
Bonds issued by a large, well-established company	?

As the above exercise should illustrate, it is generally the case that equities are more risky than bonds. This is because, unlike bonds, equities do not specify a percentage return that will be paid each year and do not have a set date at which they are repaid. Furthermore, when something goes wrong, it is the equities that are last in the queue when it comes to getting any money back.

It is also the case that when looking at two bonds, or two equities, the bonds or equities issued by the smaller, less financially secure entity are going to be more risky than the bonds or equities issued by the larger, more financially secure entity.

4. Equity and Bond Markets

Learning Objective 2.1.4

Know that the financial services sector also includes markets to enable investors in equities and bonds to buy or sell investments

As has been made clear in the preceding section, equities are different from bonds in a number of respects including the following:

• Equities give the holder an ownership stake in the issuing company. Bonds do not.

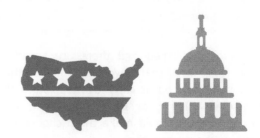

CISI
CHARTERED INSTITUTE FOR
SECURITIES & INVESTMENT

- Equities have no set date of repayment. Bonds typically have a set repayment date.
- Equities do not pay interest. Bonds typically do pay a specified percentage interest each year.

With this in mind, why are investors willing to put money into equities when they can see little or no prospect of the issuing company buying those equities back in the future? Fundamentally, they hope the company will perform well and generate profits. A share of these profits might be paid by the company to the **shareholders** in the form of **dividends** (see chapter 4, section 3), but ultimately the holders of equity know that they will be able to sell the equities they own to someone else. Selling the equities will enable them to realise their investment, potentially for more money than they paid for the shares.

Facilities to sell equities are provided by the equity markets, and include world-famous **exchanges** like the New York Stock Exchange (NYSE), the Abu Dhabi Securities Exchange (ADX) and the **London Stock Exchange (LSE)**. Most countries have stock exchanges and other examples include Singapore's SGX, Sri Lanka's Colombo Stock Exchange, India's Bombay Stock Exchange, South Africa's Johannesburg Stock Exchange (JSE) and Saudi Arabia's Tadawul. These exchanges trade millions of shares every day and began as meeting places where buyers (or people representing them) would meet sellers (or people representing them) to agree purchases and sales. Now the majority of deals are made electronically, with most exchanges essentially operating as electronic auction facilities similar to eBay.

Buyers of shares

Sellers of shares

Markets

Where deals are arranged. Known as stock exchanges.

Like equities, bonds can be bought or sold before they reach their repayment dates.

However, in contrast to equities, most bonds tend to be bought and sold away from the big exchanges. This is largely due to the fact that nearly all bonds have a maturity or repayment date when the bondholder's IOU will be repaid. For equity holders this will not happen, so a facility to sell the shares has traditionally been much more important. Those buyers of bonds that do wish to sell before the repayment date are brought together with sellers of bonds via electronic facilities that are generally described as **over-the-counter (OTC)** facilities. OTC is simply a term for trades that are arranged away from the established exchanges.

5. Insurance

Learning Objective 2.1.5
Know that the financial services sector also includes insurance providers to enable financial risks to be managed

In addition to providing the link between savers and borrowers, the financial services sector also includes activities that are best described as risk management. We all face risk in our lives, and the examples of the risks faced are numerous – from the risk of a car crash to the risk of a household burglary and the risk of suffering from a serious illness.

These and other risks can be controlled by taking out insurance from insurance companies. The insurance company will take on specified risks in exchange for a series of **premium** payments. If the risk materialises, the insurance company will pay out.

There are numerous different forms of insurance, ranging from a large shipping company covering the risks that its ships may break down or hit rocks – known as marine insurance – to a 'life policy' where an individual insures that, if they die, their dependants will receive a lump sum of money sufficient to clear the mortgage loan on the family home. Further examples are detailed below.

⚙ Example

Motor Insurance

Charlie is 21 years old and has just bought his first car – a second hand, seven-year-old but high specification Volkswagen Golf that is worth £3,000. It is a legal requirement that Charlie has insurance before he takes the car out on the road. He contacts an insurance company, which quotes him £1,200 for a one-year policy that will pay out in the event of an accident that is Charlie's fault. Charlie signs up, agreeing to pay a monthly premium of £100, and starts to enjoy driving his new car on the road.

Exercise 3 – Insurance Premiums

Charlie's mother Sarah has a two-year-old car, a BMW worth £15,000. Sarah has been driving for 20 years and has never had an accident. Her monthly premium is £50.

Why do you think Sarah's monthly premium is so much less than Charlie's, despite her car being worth more?

The answer can be found in the appendix at the end of this chapter.

⚙ Example

Oil Rig Insurance

A recently established oil exploration company – Explo inc – has just completed the construction of its first oil rig in the ocean off West Africa. The rig is estimated to be worth around $100 million and Explo wants to insure the rig in case of damage due to mechanical failure or adverse weather. An insurance company offers to insure the rig for $5 million per annum.

By taking up the offer with the insurance company, Explo's worries about mechanical and weather damage are much reduced – the

risks have been transferred to the insurance company in exchange for the premium of $5 million each year.

There are a number of substantial insurance companies in the world, including well-known names like Axa of France and Allianz of Germany. However, despite the size of an individual insurance company, the amount of risk it takes on when it sells insurance may be too big for it to be willing to bear alone.

To manage the risk, insurance companies can, and do, take out insurance themselves and this is generally referred to as **reinsurance**. Reinsurance allows the risk taken on by insurance companies to be shared.

Exercise 4 – Oil Rig Insurance

Explo inc has essentially transferred the risk of damage to the oil rig to the insurance company. Now the insurance company is facing a risk that could result in paying out $100 million if the oil rig is destroyed in a typhoon.

What could the insurance company do to reduce its risk?

The answer can be found in the appendix at the end of this chapter.

6. Foreign Exchange

Learning Objective 2.1.6
Know that the financial services sector also includes foreign exchange dealers to allow one currency to be exchanged for another to facilitate international trade

Foreign exchange (Forex, or FX) is simply changing a particular quantity of one **currency**, such as US$100, for a particular amount of another currency, such as €90.

There are a considerable number of different foreign currencies across the world, and the most obvious example of the need for foreign exchange arises whenever individuals travel to different parts of the world.

Example

When an American crosses the Atlantic and visits France for a holiday, they will need euros rather than their more familiar US dollars. To get hold of euros they will probably go to their bank in advance of the trip and purchase a couple of hundred US dollars' worth of euros. If the appropriate rate for euros per US dollar were 0.86, their $200 would get them €172.

So, individuals travelling gives rise to some foreign exchange activity, but this is dwarfed by the impact of businesses buying and selling things across borders.

Example

An American company – SurfBoards of America (SBoA) – manufactures surfboards and receives a substantial order from a European retailer that wants to pay in euros.

SBoA ships the surfboards and ends up receiving thousands of euros from the European client. However, SBoA needs US dollars, so it calls up the foreign exchange dealer at its local bank and agrees to sell the euros for the US dollars it wants.

The US dollar is regarded as the most important currency in the world, and as a result it is typical that the way foreign exchange tends to be quoted is by the number of a particular currency that a US dollar is worth. The attraction to the banks and their **dealers** of offering foreign exchange quotes is in providing services their clients need, arising from international trade and international travel in particular. The banks and their dealers will earn fees as a result. Part of the attraction to banks and dealers is that the daily activity in foreign exchange is reportedly exceeding a massive $5 trillion (that's $5,000 billion), reflecting the scale of international trade.

Exercise 5 – Where to Go Next?

*Raj is a US citizen and has two great loves – seeing the world and enjoying his favourite creamy cappuccino coffee. He is trying to decide which capital city he will visit next, and has decided to go to the one with the cheapest cappuccino in US dollar terms. His local café in New York sells large cappuccinos for $5. Below, are the local currency prices in the ten cities that Raj is considering. Using either newspapers or the internet, please find the relevant **exchange rates** and calculate the equivalent US dollar price. Then rank the cities from the cheapest to the most expensive cappuccino. The answer is provided in the appendix at the end of this chapter, and the rates detailed there are as at January 2019.*

City and currency	Cappuccino price in local currency	Exchange rate with the US dollar	Equivalent US dollar price	Ranking: cheapest (1) to most expensive (10)
Rio – Brazilian reals	9.00		2.15	
Hong Kong – Hong Kong dollars	42.50		5.6	
Mumbai – Indian rupees	240.00		3.36	
Tokyo – Japanese yen	500.00		4.58	
Paris – euros	4.00		4.4	
London – UK pounds	4.00		5.2	
Dubai – UAE dirham	18.00		4.63	

Jeddah – Saudi Arabian riyals	22.00		5.96	
Zurich – Swiss francs	5.50		5.66	
Moscow – Russian roubles	210.00			

Exercise 6

If a company borrows money by issuing IOUs ('I owe you') in return for the money loaned, how are these IOUs typically described?

a. Shares
b. Bonds
c. Equity
d. Loans

Exercise 7

Certain governments, such as the US and the UK, have substantial amounts of national debt. How is this national debt usually funded?

a. Using equity
b. Using bonds
c. Using loans
d. Using shares

Exercise 8

If the holder of a bond wants to realise their investment before the scheduled repayment date, which of the following would they normally do?

a. Arrange an early repayment with the bond issuer
b. Exchange the bond for equities
c. Sell the bond on the stock market
d. Sell the bond OTC

⚙ Answers to Chapter Exercises

Exercise 1 – Financing Choices

Consideration	Borrowing or Equity?
Which one is more expensive (in terms of annual cash costs)?	**Answer: Borrowing** Borrowing is the more expensive in terms of the requirement to pay interest each year. Equity does not require the payment of interest.
Which one is likely to need to be repaid earlier?	**Answer: Borrowing** Borrowing is generally required to be repaid on, or by, an agreed future date. There is no such requirement in relation to shares.
Which one is more likely to be available for a start-up company?	**Answer: Equity** Since a start-up has not established a pattern of making money, borrowing is often unavailable. However, equity finance may be available from investors who are willing to take a risk in the hope of making a substantial return if the start-up is successful. Furthermore, governments often provide incentives for equity investors in early-stage and start-up companies that enable them to save some tax. The logic of the incentives is to encourage job creation and increase the attractiveness of investing in the equity of start-ups.
Which one is likely to be the more risky for the finance provider?	**Answer: Equity** If the company is a start-up, then both forms of finance are risky. The business may not succeed and has not yet proved itself. However, if the business does get off the ground, but is not particularly successful, the providers of borrowed finance will at least receive some interest. It is also the case that if the company does fail and there is any money left at all, the borrowing is repaid before the equity. So, equity is more risky because it is the last in the queue, standing behind borrowings in terms of the order of repayment.
Which one is likely to have the largest potential 'upside' for the finance provider?	**Answer: Equity** When a company does spectacularly well, it is the shareholders (as owners) who will benefit. There are numerous stories of technology billionaires who provided equity to companies like Microsoft®, Google, Facebook and Alibaba. By contrast, the upside for those banks that have provided borrowed finance to successful start-ups is simply to get the interest and to be repaid in full.

Based on the above, can you understand why CareerComic chose to raise finance through equity?

For CareerComic, borrowing might not have been available, and even if it were available it would mean CareerComic would need to find the cash to pay the interest and ultimately to repay the money. Equity finance will not demand the payment of interest and, from the finance provider's perspective, provides the upside potential that could run into thousands, millions or even billions.

Exercise 2 – Risk and Reward

Suggesed order, from the most risky (and potentially rewarding) to the least risky (and safer).

Investments	Risk ranking (where 1 is the highest risk and 6 the lowest risk)
US government bonds	6
Equities issued by a start-up company	2
Equities issued by a large, well-established company	3
Bonds issued by a large, well-established company	4
Bank account	5
Roulette wheel at a casino	1

Note: It is debatable whether money invested in US government bonds faces less risk than a bank account. Some would argue that the US government bonds are safest, as they are denominated in US dollars and the US prints the dollars. A bank could collapse, and the depositor might lose money as a result. This view is taken in the above suggested answer.

However, bank balances within certain limits are typically provided with insurance in the form of a government guarantee. If the bank account is assumed to be within the government's insurance limits, it could be considered to be at the same risk ranking as the government's bonds. Furthermore, since the US occasionally suffers from political infighting when its borrowing is approaching certain limits (known as the 'debt ceiling'), it could be that the bank account is considered less risky than the government bonds. The real world is not quite as straightforward as we might like!

Exercise 3 – Insurance Premiums

Charlie is 21 years old and he has just bought his first car – a seven-year-old VW Golf that is worth £3,000. His insurance costs him £1,200 for one year – £100 per month. Charlie's mother Sarah has a two-year-old car, a BMW worth £15,000. Sarah has been driving for 20 years and has never had an accident. Her monthly premium is £50.

The reason Sarah's monthly premium is only half the amount of Charlie's, despite her car being worth much more, is all about risk. The insurance company judges the likelihood of Charlie having an accident as much greater than the likelihood of Sarah having an accident. The reasons include the fact that Charlie is a young, inexperienced male driver, and such drivers have a history of driving too fast and being involved in a significant number of road accidents.

By contrast, Sarah has already proven to be accident-free for the last 20 years and is a far more experienced driver. Middle-aged women tend to be involved in far fewer road accidents than young males.

So, the likelihood of the insurance company being required to pay out on a claim for Sarah is deemed to be much less than for Charlie. Despite the relative values of the cars, the insurance company deems the risk and size of possible payout to be less for Sarah than for Charlie.

Exercise 4 – Oil Rig Insurance

Explo inc has transferred the risk of damage of an oil rig worth $100 million to the insurance company. The insurance company is facing a risk that could result in it paying out $100 million if the oil rig is destroyed in a typhoon or another incident.

If this is deemed to be too large a risk for the insurance company to bear, the solution is for the insurance company to share the risk by taking out insurance with other insurers. This often happens and is called reinsurance. The insurer of Explo's $100 million oil rig is likely to reinsure a significant portion of this, such as $90 million, with other insurers. This would subsequently leave Explo with just $10 million of risk, a sum that it can handle with more ease.

Exercise 5 – Where To Go Next?

Based on the exchange rates in January 2019, Raj should choose Rio for his next visit, as a cappuccino there is the cheapest in US dollar terms at $2.42. This is significantly cheaper than Raj pays in his local New York café, where the price is $5.

City and currency	Cappuccino price in local currency	Exchange rate with the US dollar	Equivalent US dollar price	Ranking: cheapest (1) to most expensive (10)
Rio – Brazilian reals	9.00	3.7176	2.42	1
Hong Kong – Hong Kong dollars	42.50	7.8444	5.42	8
Mumbai – Indian rupees	240.00	71.167	3.37	3
Tokyo – Japanese yen	500.00	108.61	4.60	5
Paris – euros	4.00	0.8773	4.56	4
London – UK pounds	4.00	0.7771	5.15	7
Dubai – UAE dirham	18.00	3.6725	4.90	6
Jeddah – Saudi Arabian riyals	22.00	3.7500	5.87	10
Zurich – Swiss francs	5.50	0.9891	5.56	9
Moscow – Russian roubles	210.00	66.7778	3.14	2

Exercise 6 – Bonds

6. B (chapter 2, section 1.3).

Bonds are effectively IOUs issued by organisations such as companies and governments in return for money for a period of time.

Exercise 7 – National Debt

7. B (chapter 2, section 2).

National debt is generally funded by the issue of government bonds.

Exercise 8 – OTC Facilities

8. D (chapter 2, section 4).

The vast majority of bonds that are sold before the scheduled repayment date are traded away from established exchanges on OTC facilities.

Banking

3

This syllabus area will provide approximately 5 of the 30 examination questions

Fundamentals of Financial Services

Banking

This chapter will focus on banks – what they do and in particular how the various types of bank differ from one another. As already mentioned in chapter 2, part of the complexity that appears to be present within financial services is simply the result of the jargon that is invariably used. We will unravel and explain the special language that is used in banking in this chapter.

1. Retail and Commercial Banking

Learning Objective 3.1.1

Know the difference between retail and commercial banking and the types of customer – individuals/corporates

Most of us are aware of what **retail banks** do, because we see them on the high street. Individuals are often referred to as retail

customers, and banks that provide services to individuals are referred to as retail banks. The business model for a retail bank is similar to the business model that was introduced in the previous chapter – the bank will try to attract deposits from individuals, and use these deposits to make loans to other individuals. The bank should generate a surplus because the interest it pays on deposits is less than the interest it demands on loans. This surplus can then be used by the bank to pay its other expenses, such as paying the wages of the staff and the rental on the premises. If a surplus still remains after paying all of these other expenses, the bank has generated a profit.

The term commercial bank is often encountered in the financial services sector, especially in the US. It is used in one of two contexts. The US uses it as a term that captures all the banks that are doing what has thus far been referred to as the activities of a bank: attracting deposits and making loans. In other parts of the world, the term 'commercial banking' is often used to isolate those banks that specialise in providing banking facilities (deposits and loans) to commercial entities, in other words to businesses, rather than individuals.

This latter definition is alternatively described as corporate banking, since the business clients are predominantly corporate entities, ie, companies.

Commercial Banks

The US definition – all banks that take deposits and grant loans

Retail Banks

Banks that specialise in taking deposits and providing loans to individuals

Corporate Banks

Banks that specialise in taking deposits and providing loans to businesses. In parts of the world outside the US, these are often referred to as commercial banks

It can be a little misleading to refer to banks as retail or commercial, since the reality is that most banks do both. Just think of the likes of Bank of America in the US, Lloyds and Barclays in the UK and HSBC globally, where both retail and corporate clients are catered for.

2. Retail Borrowing in Focus

Learning Objective 3.1.2

Know the nature and types of borrowing available to retail customers: from banks – loans, mortgage loans, overdrafts; from banks and credit card companies – credit cards; from other sources – pawnbrokers, payday loans

Individuals sometimes like, or even need, to spend more money than they have by borrowing. The bank is often the first place they go to in order to borrow money, as they tend to deposit their funds in retail bank accounts.

2.1 Loans, Mortgages and Overdrafts

The three most common forms of borrowing provided to retail customers by banks are loans, mortgages and overdrafts. Each of these are illustrated in the examples below.

⚙ Example

Three college graduates – Dot, Jade and Anna – have started working full-time.

Dot's job is some distance from her home and public transport is not great, so she decides that she needs to buy a car. She finds an ideal vehicle, a second-hand Volkswagen Polo that will cost around $6,000.

As Dot has little in the way of savings, she applies to her bank for a $6,000 loan. The terms are that the loan will be repaid in monthly instalments over three years, and interest will be charged at 8% per annum.

The above example saw Dot borrow money for the car purchase using a bank loan. Bank loans can be taken out for any purpose – it doesn't have to be for a car – but the standard features are that the loan is normally:

- for a set period that is generally less than five years (it is three years in the above example)
- at a set rate of interest (8% in the above example)
- with a defined repayment schedule (monthly in the above example).

Dot's loan is also called an **unsecured** loan. This is because the bank does not require any **security**, such as the car, to be handed over to it while the loan is outstanding.

Jade is fortunate enough to have wealthy parents who have encouraged her to buy a home of her own. Jade has found a property that is ideal, but it will cost her $250,000. Her parents have agreed to give her $50,000 and she borrows the rest from the bank in the form of a mortgage.

The terms are that Jade will make monthly repayments over 25 years; the interest rate for the loan will be at the bank's standard variable rate (currently 6%, but liable to change) and, in the event of Jade failing to make the required payments, the bank has the ability to take ownership of the property in order to recoup the money owed.

The above example is a mortgage loan, often just described as a mortgage. Mortgage loans are always taken out to buy property, and because they tend to involve substantial sums of money, the loans are generally repaid over longer periods than other forms of loan. Since the bank that lends the money will be repaid over this lengthy period, the bank tends to charge a variable rate of interest that can increase or decrease to stay in line with general interest rates.

Furthermore, unlike most other forms of loan, the mortgage loan has the safety feature for the bank that it is **secured** on the property. If the borrower fails to make the scheduled repayments, the bank can take the property in order to repay the loan. Other loans tend not to have the same feature and are described as unsecured.

In summary, mortgages are typically:

- for a set period (25 years in the above example)
- at a variable rate of interest (the bank's 'standard variable rate' in the above example)
- with a defined repayment schedule (monthly in the above example)
- secured on the property the loan is used to buy.

Anna is a writer and her income varies. Some months she earns a lot, but in the summer months she prefers to travel rather than write, so her income falls. Anna enjoys food and loves nothing more than a good meal at a restaurant. In fact, she is so keen on eating out that in some months the habit is costing her more than the money she is earning. Because of her variable income, Anna has an agreement with her bank that she is allowed to spend up to $1,000 more money than she has in her account, mostly in the lean summers. This is described as an overdraft facility. There is no set date or schedule for repayment; however, the bank is able to remove this facility whenever it wishes. There is the expectation that Anna will be able to repay the overdraft during the busier winter months. The bank will charge Anna an overdraft rate that is currently 10% per annum, but this can be changed at any time as long as the bank gives Anna at least 14 days' notice. Anna also has to pay a one-off or annual arrangement fee of $50 to the bank to start the overdraft facility.

The above example is a typical overdraft facility. Overdrafts are flexible, so Anna can use as much or as little of the $1,000 as she needs. She can also repay the overdraft and then draw cash from the facility again at a later date. However, the lending bank can technically demand repayment at any time, although it would be unlikely to do so. Overdrafts are also relatively expensive in terms of the interest rate they charge, and may also incur a fee for the facility being set up (known as an arrangement fee).

In summary, bank overdrafts are generally:

- flexible – able to be drawn, repaid, drawn again up to the overdraft limit ($1,000 in the above example)
- at a variable rate of interest (the bank's overdraft rate in the above example), an arrangement fee may also be payable ($50 in the above example)
- unsecured and repayable on demand.

Forms of Retail Borrowing from Banks

Loans
- fixed term
- set interest rate
- agreed repay-
  ment schedule
- unsecured

Mortgage Loans
- fixed term
- agreed repayment
  schedule
- secured on the
  property

Overdrafts
- repayable on
  demand
- variable interest
  rate
- no set repayment
  schedule
- unsecured

2.2 Credit Cards

Borrowing that is even more flexible than an overdraft is often available through credit cards. Credit cards are available from banks, as well as specialist providers like Visa and MasterCard and even through supermarkets, football clubs and charities.

The way a credit card works is that an individual applies for a card and, if successful, is granted a card with a certain borrowing limit (the credit limit). They can then use the card to purchase things and with each purchase the amount borrowed will increase. At least part of the borrowed money needs to be paid off monthly. Generally, the borrowed money that is not paid off incurs a hefty amount of interest, usually around 20% per annum, so it is a good idea to pay off all of the borrowed money each month to avoid any interest being charged.

So, credit cards typically have the following characteristics:

- flexible – able to be used up to the credit limit
- at a variable rate of interest, which tends to be expensive
- repayments of at least a minimum amount are required monthly.

2.3 Other Sources

For individuals who are somewhat desperate to borrow money – often where the banks and credit card issuers have already reached the maximum lending available – other options exist in the form of **pawnbrokers** and **payday loans**. To obtain a loan from a pawnbroker, something of value is required that provides

the pawnbroker with some security. This might be a wedding ring or another valuable piece of jewellery, such as a watch. The security needs to be something of value (real, sentimental or both) that the pawnbroker can hold and store until the loan is repaid. The decision on the loan is usually made immediately by the pawnbroker. Invariably, the interest rate charged on borrowing from a pawnbroker is much greater than borrowing from a bank or on a credit card.

Exercise 1 – Pawnbroker Loans

Why do you think a loan from the pawnbroker is more expensive than a loan or overdraft from a bank, or borrowing on a credit card?

The answer can be found in the appendix at the end of this chapter.

Payday loans are marketed as loans that enable the borrower to get hold of cash before the next time they are paid by their employer. They are a very expensive form of borrowing, but the offer is a very simple one, as shown in the example below.

⚙ Example

A payday loan provider offers Mr Short the ability to 'borrow up to £1,000 now'. It is true that the lender will make an immediate decision, but the bad news is that the loan also comes at a cost: '£16.80 per £100'. The terms also require repayment at Mr Short's next pay date, which is only three weeks away. So the cost of borrowing is 16.8% for a period of just 21 days, which equates to around 292% per annum!

However, because of a public outcry over the high rates of interest charged, in some countries, such as the UK, the regulator has imposed a limit on the rate of interest that can be charged. Since January 2015, UK-based payday lenders can now charge no more than 0.8% per day.

In summary, loans from pawnbrokers and payday loans are:

- easily available – the decisions tend to be made immediately
- relatively very expensive in comparison to other forms of borrowing
- for pawned items, repayment is required to regain possession of the pawned item from the pawnbroker
- for payday loans, loans are very short-term, with repayment required at the next payday.

Other Forms of Borrowing

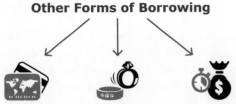

Credit Cards	Pawnbrokers	Payday Loans
– flexible	– requires valuable(s) to be left as security (pawned)	– borrower needs to be employed
– variable interest rate	– immediate decision	– repayable on next payday
– minimum payment required each month	– expensive	– immediate decision
– unsecured		– expensive

3. Interest Rates

Learning Objective 3.1.3

Know the difference between the quoted interest rate on borrowing and the effective annual rate of borrowing

When borrowing money, it is normal for the lender to charge interest. The lender might be a bank, a credit card company or even a payday loan company. The way the interest rate is disclosed could potentially be rather misleading.

Here are some fictional examples:

⚙ Example

Tom is looking to borrow some money to buy a new laptop; he has found four alternative sources:

1. *ABC bank is offering a personal loan that will charge interest at 10% per annum, with the interest being added to the loan each quarter.*

2. *XYZ bank is offering a loan that will charge interest at 10% per annum, with the interest being added to the loan each month.*
3. *The MISA credit card will charge interest at 1% each month.*
4. *The Payday Loan Company will charge interest at 0.8% each day.*

Which is the cheapest source of finance for Tom?

On a superficial basis, the two lower quotes (the credit card and the payday loan) might seem cheaper than the 10% quotes from the banks. However, it is pretty clear that the payday loan is the most expensive despite only quoting 0.8%, because the percentage is a daily rate. It can immediately be calculated as more like 292% per annum (as there are 365 days most years).

Similarly, but nowhere near as excessively, the MISA credit card looks expensive compared to the two banks. The banks are both quoting 10%, and a monthly charge of 1% can immediately be thought of as around 12% per annum, as there are 12 months in each year.

So, Tom is left with the choice of ABC or XYZ, each quoting 10%. However, there is a clear winner here – ABC bank is cheaper because it charges interest every quarter, whereas XYZ adds it every month. This means that the balance on the loan increases every month at XYZ bank but only every quarter at ABC bank. Interest is charged on the outstanding balance, so, in effect, interest is being charged on interest more frequently at XYZ bank. This is shown below if we assume Tom borrows $1,000 and we look at how the balance on the loan increases in the two banks over the first six months.

ABC Bank

The quarterly interest rate that is added to the loan is the annual rate of 10% divided by the four quarters in the year = 10%/4 = 2.5%.

Date	Opening balance ($)	Interest ($)	Closing balance ($)
End of month 1	1,000.00	–	1,000.00
End of month 2	1,000.00	–	1,000.00
End of month 3	1,000.00	25.00	1,025.00
End of month 4	1,025.00	–	1,025.00
End of month 5	1,025.00	–	1,025.00
End of month 6	1,025.00	25.625	1,050.625

XYZ Bank

The monthly interest rate that is added to the loan is the annual rate of 10% divided by the 12 months in the year = 10%/12 = 0.833%.

Date	Opening balance ($)	Interest ($)	Closing balance ($)
End of month 1	1,000.00	8.33	1,008.33
End of month 2	1,008.33	8.40	1,016.73
End of month 3	1,016.73	8.47	1,025.20
End of month 4	1,025.20	8.54	1,033.74
End of month 5	1,033.74	8.61	1,042.35
End of month 6	1,042.35	8.68	1,051.03

So, after six months it is clear from the above that ABC bank is cheaper, with a loan balance of $1,050.625 compared to the larger loan balance of $1,051.03 at XYZ. This is because ABC is charging interest less frequently (quarterly compared to XYZ's monthly).

The above example shows that the way interest is disclosed could be misleading unless care is taken to make sure everything is taken into account. In reality, the regulatory authorities help too by requiring lenders to quote rates on a comparable basis. Generally the quoted rate has to be made available on an annual basis, and some form of **effective annual rate** is also disclosed. The effective annual rate takes the quoted rate and adjusts it to take into account the frequency of interest charges. If the frequency of charging interest is annually, the quoted rate and the effective annual rate are the same. When interest is charged more frequently than annually – for example quarterly, or monthly – the effective annual rate will be greater than the quoted rate.

Below is the detail from the earlier example presented with both annual quoted rates and effective annual rates, making the cheapest option much more straightforward to isolate.

⚙ Example

Lender and detail	Quoted rate (pa)	Effective annual rate
ABC bank – interest 10% per annum, each quarter	10%	10.38%
XYZ bank – interest 10% per annum, each month	10%	10.47%
MISA credit card – interest at 1% each month	12%	12.68%
Payday Loan Company – interest at 0.8% each day	292%	1,365%

As the table shows, the quoted rate on an annual basis begins to identify the more expensive options immediately, particularly the Payday Loan Company's 292%. However, it is the effective annual rate that shows just how expensive the payday loan is compared to all of the others at well over 1,360%! The effective annual rate also clearly shows that the ABC bank option is the cheapest, since, despite having the same quoted rate as XYZ bank, the interest is charged less frequently.

In summary, when comparing the cost of borrowing, it is sensible to:

- look at the annual quoted percentages, rather than quarterly, monthly, weekly or daily percentages
- look for the effective annual rates to make a true comparison, including the impact of how often the interest is charged.

3.1 Calculating the Effective Annual Rate

Learning Objective 3.1.4

Be able to calculate the effective annual rate given the quoted rate and frequency of interest payment

The annual quoted percentage on borrowing can be very different from the effective annual rate of borrowing, as illustrated in the earlier example. Calculating the effective annual rate from the annual quoted percentage can be done in the following way:

⚙ Example

Returning to the earlier example of a loan from ABC bank that charges interest each quarter based on a quoted rate of 10% per annum:

Step 1: *Calculate the interest rate charged for each period specified by the loan.*

The loan is charged interest quarterly, so the interest rate charged each quarter is the annual rate of 10% divided by 4 (because there are four quarters in each year).

Interest charged each quarter = 10% ÷ 4 = 2.5% each quarter

Step 2: *Assuming a loan of £100 at the start of the year, calculate how much will be owed at the end of the year using the rate calculated in Step 1 and assuming no interest is paid during the year.*

Starting balance on the loan at the beginning of the year = £100.

Interest charged at the end of the first quarter = 100 x 2.5% = £2.50.

Starting balance on the loan at the start of the second quarter (assuming no interest has been paid) = £100 + £2.50 = £102.50.

Interest charged at the end of the second quarter = £102.50 x 2.5% = £2.56 (rounded to the nearest penny).

Starting balance on the loan at the start of the third quarter (assuming no interest has been paid) = £102.50 + £2.56 = £105.06.

Interest charged at the end of the third quarter = £105.06 x 2.5% = £2.63 (rounded to the nearest penny).

Starting balance on the loan at the start of the fourth quarter (assuming no interest has been paid) = £105.06 + £2.63 = £107.69.

Interest charged at the end of the fourth quarter = £107.69 x 2.5% = £2.69 (rounded to the nearest penny).

Balance on the loan at the end of the year (assuming no interest has been paid) = £107.69 + £2.69 = £110.38.

Step 3: *Using the end balance on the loan calculated in Step 2, work out the effective interest charged for the year.*

Ending balance less starting balance = £110.38 – £100.00 = £10.38 effective interest charged over the year.

Step 4: *Express the effective interest charged as a percentage of the starting balance to give the effective annual rate.*

Effective interest divided by starting balance = £10.38 ÷ £100.00 = 0.1038.

Multiplied by 100 to give a percentage = 0.1038 x 100 = 10.38%.

NOTE: *UK sterling (pounds or £) are divided into 100 pence, singular penny, also written 'p'. US dollars ($) are divided into 100 cents, also written 'c' or '¢'.*

Exercise 2 – Calculating the Effective Annual Rate

Greenboot Bank is offering a loan at a quoted rate of 2% per month (that's 24% per annum). What is the effective annual rate?

The answer can be found in the appendix to this chapter.

Using the approach detailed above to answer Exercise 2 is quite a task when the interest is charged to the account each month, needing a total of 12 calculations. Imagine if the quoted rate were charged on a weekly or daily basis – that would mean 52 or 365 calculations!

Thankfully, there is an alternative approach that can handle more frequent charges without the need to perform multiple calculations. This alternative approach is detailed below using the earlier example of 10% charged quarterly.

⚙ Example

Alternative approach to calculating the effective annual rate:

Step 1: *Calculate the interest rate charged for each period specified by the loan.*

This is 10% per annum, charged quarterly. Since there are four quarters in a year the rate is 10/4 = 2.5% each quarter.

Step 2: *Express the rate from Step 1 as a decimal, by dividing it by 100.*

2.5/100 is 0.025.

Step 3: *Add the number 1 to the result from Step 2 and multiply it by itself by the number of times interest will be charged over the year.*

1 + 0.025 = 1.025.

1.025 multiplied by itself four times (since interest is charged quarterly) = 1.025^4 = 1.1038.

Note: 1.025^4 (1.025 'to the power of 4') is another way of expressing 1.025 x 1.025 x 1.025 x 1.025.

Step 4: *Deduct 1 from the result of Step 3 and express the result as a percentage by multiplying it by 100.*

1.1038 – 1 = 0.1038
0.1038 x 100 = 10.38%.

Exercise 3 – Effective Annual Rate Calculation Using an Alternative Approach

Please try to calculate the effective annual rate for Greenboot Bank's loan that charges 2% each month using the alternative approach.

The answer can be found in the appendix at the end of this chapter.

4. Secured and Unsecured Borrowing

Learning Objective 3.1.5

Know the difference between secured and unsecured borrowing

Earlier in this chapter (in section 2), a number of sources of borrowing were encountered of which two in particular were identified as secured borrowing. Secured borrowing is where the lender has the right to take something that belongs to the borrower if the borrower fails to meet the terms of the loan. This is also known as the lender 'taking security'.

The most obvious example of secured borrowing is when an individual raises a loan to buy a home – a mortgage. It is normal for the lender to assess the value of the property being purchased before granting the loan, and to restrict the loan to a percentage of that value. The rationale is best illustrated by looking at an example.

Fundamentals of Financial Services

Example

Jade is buying a property that will cost her $250,000. The bank has agreed the value to be $250,000 and is willing to lend 80% of the value to Jade. In the event of Jade failing to make the required payments, the bank has the right to take ownership of the property in order to recoup the money owed.

The reason that lenders such as banks want the security of the property is that, in the event of financial hardship for the borrower, the bank can take and sell the property if it needs to and, since it has only loaned a proportion of the value (80% in the above example), the bank has a reasonable safety net against property prices falling. Of course, since it is a safer loan for the bank because of the security, it is also a cheaper loan for the borrower.

Exercise 4 – The Value of a Bank's Security

How much must the value of the house Jade is buying fall, before the bank has no security?

The answer can be found in the appendix to this chapter.

It is not only mortgage loans that are secured. We encountered pawnbrokers earlier that also provide a form of secured loan. Furthermore, companies that need to borrow money generally may be able to borrow more cheaply by offering some of their **assets** as security. The company's assets might include land and buildings.

If a loan is not secured, it is described as unsecured. Generally, unsecured loans are more expensive than secured loans because the risk to the lender is greater.

5. The Relative Cost of Borrowing

Learning Objective 3.1.6
Know what types of borrowing are likely to be relatively expensive – pawnbrokers/payday loans, credit cards, overdrafts, unsecured loans; and cheaper – secured loans, eg, mortgages

The previous sections have highlighted the relative costs of various forms of borrowing. The following exercise will explore and reinforce these costs further:

Exercise 5 – Which Form of Borrowing is Cheapest?

Try to rank the borrowing taken by the various individuals from the cheapest to the most expensive. Once completed, review the suggested answer and explanations at the end of the chapter.

Borrowing source	Ranking (1 = cheapest, 6 = most expensive)
Greg is in great need of cash, having exhausted most sources and being unemployed. He manages to find a pawnbroker willing to lend him $2,000, but he has to deposit his wife's wedding ring with the pawnbroker.	
Aaron is a reasonably well-paid office worker who has saved up enough cash to enable him to pay 10% of the purchase price of a $200,000 flat. The remainder will come from a bank in the form of a mortgage loan.	

Maya is a trainee solicitor and has just rented her first flat. Unfortunately, the flat is lacking a washing machine and Maya is borrowing $1,000 in the form of an unsecured loan from a bank to enable her to buy a washing machine and have it plumbed in.	
Zeenat is 25 years old and is a very capable musician. She is self-employed and tends to be particularly busy in the winter season in theatre orchestras. To cover the seasonal nature of her earnings, she has arranged a $1,500 overdraft facility with her bank.	
Rajiv is 30 and is trying very hard to establish a business as a DJ. He has a regular slot at a nightclub in his local town, and in order to widen his appeal he is planning to purchase some new equipment that will cost around $1,200. Rajiv decides that the best way to fund the purchase is to buy the equipment on his credit card, which he hopes he will be in a position to repay in full in six months or so.	
Mohammed is employed, but has got himself into a financial mess with his love of expensive holidays. He is finding it very difficult to get any more borrowing from his bank or his credit card providers. He has decided to borrow $500 in the form of a payday loan that will cover him until he gets paid in two weeks.	

It is generally cheaper to borrow on a secured basis than on an unsecured basis. A bank will invariably offer mortgage loans at a lower interest rate than an unsecured loan to the same borrower. This ties back to the idea of risk and reward – for the lender, secured borrowing provides a safety net, so there is less risk. If there is less risk, the lender will accept less reward.

6. Investment Banks

Learning Objective 3.1.7

Know that investment banks help companies to raise money and advise them on strategy, eg, mergers and acquisitions

Banks have been repeatedly mentioned in the first two chapters. However, two types of banks have not yet been expanded upon – **investment banks** and **central banks**.

Investment banks are not like the deposit-taking banks encountered so far. They are specialists in what is commonly referred to as 'capital-raising', and particularly in large-scale capital-raising, starting at around £5 million and upwards to around £100 billion. Capital is long-term finance and is required by companies and many governments. Broadly, it comes in two forms – equity and debt (bonds or loans). So, when a company is looking to raise long-term finance, it will go to an investment bank for advice. The investment bank might recommend equity, it may recommend debt or perhaps a combination of both.

Presuming the company elects to go ahead, the investment bank will make it happen – 'executing the deal' in the jargon of the markets – by putting together the required paperwork and marketing the deal to potential investors.

In addition to helping organisations raise capital, another major line of business for investment banks is **mergers** and **acquisitions** (M&A). This is where investment banks advise companies on their business strategy, in particular on how the companies can grow by buying other businesses.

The following example is fictional, but illustrates the typical activities of an investment bank:

⚙ Example

Razak inc is already a large global player in technology that supports smartphones. Razak uses the advice of Coldman Jones, an investment bank. Coldman's M&A team recommends that Razak should buy a minor competitor company to gain access to the Japanese market. The Japanese company will cost around $100 million.

The cost of purchase needs to be raised by Razak and, again on the advice of the investment bank, Razak uses Coldman Jones to raise the required funds by selling bonds to investors.

In the above example, the investment bank recommended that Razak raise money by borrowing. This is generally referred to as debt and could have been raised by taking a loan from a bank or by issuing bonds to investors. The choice of loans or bonds is often a matter of how much the banks are keen to lend. When banks have plentiful funds, they tend to be willing and able to lend at competitive interest rates. When the banks are less willing to lend, companies that want to borrow have little choice other than the bond market.

The alternative is equity, which involves issuing shares. Let's briefly consider in which circumstances debt might be considered to be a more appropriate way to raise capital, and when equity might be more appropriate. There is no hard-and-fast rule – it is ultimately a matter of judgement – but there are circumstances that make debt more or less appropriate.

- If the company is raising the finance for something that can easily be sold, then borrowing might be more appropriate because the asset being purchased can be used as security against the loan. Property is perhaps the most obvious example for this. It tends to retain most if not all of its value and can be sold relatively easily to enable the borrowed money to be repaid.

Furthermore, if required, property can be rented out to generate funds that might cover the interest on the money borrowed.

- By contrast, when finance is being raised for items that are more inherently risky, such as a pharmaceuticals company raising capital to research a potential cure for cancer, equity tends to be the more logical choice. The outcome of the research is uncertain, and, if it does not work out, paying interest and then repaying the money may become difficult for the borrowing company. By raising equity, there is no obligation to repay, and dividends on equity are unlike interest, in that there is no requirement to pay dividends at all.

Companies choose to have a particular proportion of their capital in the form of debt and, when any of the existing debt is repaid, the company will replace it with new debt. This will mean that the company retains the same proportion of debt capital to equity capital.

Exercise 6 – The Trivandrum Tigers and Culchester United

The Trivandrum Tigers is an Indian cricket club that has grown rapidly and is hoping to finally reach Premier League status. It feels it needs to raise more money (around $50 million) to attract the best stars to the team and is considering where to get the finance. The Tigers want your advice as to how to raise the money.

Culchester United is a well-established UK football team that has just reached the top division. The football it plays is very fast and innovative, but it currently shares a ground with another London team. It owns a site in West London with permission to build, and wants to construct its own football stadium combined with a residential development. Culchester United is looking for advice on how to raise the £1 billion that will be required.

Once you have considered the above, take a look at the suggested answer in the appendix at the end of the chapter.

Investment banks are either stand-alone entities, of which some of the more well-known include Morgan Stanley and Goldman Sachs, or they are divisions of larger financial services companies that often include commercial banks, such as Deutsche Bank of Germany, or Switzerland's UBS and Credit Suisse.

7. Central Banks

Learning Objective 3.1.8

Know the role of central banks: banker to banking system; banker for the government; regulatory role (interest rate setting)

Central banks should be familiar in name at least – the Bank of England is the UK's central bank, the Federal Reserve is the central bank of the US, and Europe has its own European Central Bank. This is not a comprehensive list; almost every country in the world has its own central bank.

What do these central banks do? Despite minor differences in their role, their main functions are threefold:

The Three Main Activities of Central Banks

Banker to the Banks
– Banks hold accounts with the central bank

Banker for the Government
– The government gathers tax receipts, spends on defence and welfare
– Many governments also hold money in other currencies – foreign exchange reserves

Regulatory Role
– Many central banks regulate other banks
– Set interest rates in accordance with government policy

Looking at each function in turn:

- As **banker to the banks**, it is the central bank that holds the cash reserves of the various banks. When a cheque is drawn from one person's bank account with Citigroup and paid into another person's bank account with HSBC, the money moves across the two banks via their accounts at the central bank. Central banks also occasionally need to act as 'lender of last resort' to banks that are in temporary financial difficulties.

- As **banker for the government**, the central bank will accumulate the nation's tax receipts, and payments to the various government departments, such as health and defence, will be drawn from accounts in the central bank. As well as holding the country's foreign currency reserves, the majority of central banks also issue notes and coins on behalf of the government and manage the government debt.

- In its **regulatory role**, it is the central bank that licenses banks to operate and subsequently oversees their activities. Additionally, the central bank often has the responsibility of setting the appropriate interest rate in order to control inflation.

Mini-Assignment

Use the internet to discover a little more detail about the activities of the central bank where you are based. In particular:

1. *What is it called?*

2. *Where is it located?*

3. *How long has it been established?*

4. *Who leads the bank and how much financial experience does this person have?*

5. *Does it act as any or all of the following?*

   a. *Banker to the banks.*

   b. *Banker for the government.*

   c. *Regulator of the banks.*

Exercise 7

Which of the following is typically used by retail customers to borrow money to fund the purchase of a home?

a.   Bank loan
b.   Overdraft
c.   Mortgage
d.   Payday loan

Exercise 8

A bank is quoting a rate of borrowing on a loan at 10% annually, charged quarterly. Which of the following statements is true of the effective annual rate on the loan?

a.   It is 10%
b.   It is greater than 10%
c.   It is less than 10%
d.   It is impossible to calculate without more information

Exercise 9

What is the effective annual rate for a loan with interest charged at 12% per annum on a monthly basis?

a.   1%
b.   12%
c.   12.68%
d.   14%

Exercise 10

What type of bank typically specialises in helping companies raise money and advising them on strategy including M&A opportunities?

a.   Central bank
b.   Commercial bank
c.   Corporate bank
d.   Investment bank

Exercise 11

What type of bank is typically described as the banker to the banks?

a.   Central bank
b.   Commercial bank
c.   Corporate bank
d.   Investment bank

⚙ Answers to Chapter Exercises

Exercise 1 – Pawnbroker Loans

The reason that a loan from the pawnbroker is more expensive than a loan or overdraft from a bank comes down to the risk being borne by the pawnbroker, combined with the desperation of the borrower.

The pawnbroker typically knows very little about the borrower, other than that the borrower needs cash urgently and is willing to leave something of value as security. The borrower could take the money and never be seen again, while the security may turn out to have little value, or to be stolen! So, from the pawnbroker's standpoint, they are taking a substantial risk and want to be rewarded with a reasonable return.

Similarly, the borrower's need to go to the pawnbroker for a loan indicates that they have a pressing need for cash, cannot find it easily elsewhere and are therefore forced to pay a higher rate of interest than on other forms of loan.

Exercise 2 – Calculating the Effective Annual Rate

Greenboot Bank loan at a quoted rate of 2% per month. The effective annual rate can be calculated as follows:

Step 1: *Calculate the interest rate charged for each period specified by the loan.*

This is given as 2% per month. It can also be calculated by dividing the annual quoted rate of 24% by 12 (because there are 12 months in each year).

Step 2: *Assuming a loan of £100 at the start of the year, calculate how much will be owed at the end of the year using the rate calculated in Step 1 and assuming no interest is paid during the year.*

Starting balance on the loan at the beginning of the year = £100

Interest charged at the end of the first month = 100 x 2% = £2.00

Starting balance on the loan at the start of the second month (assuming no interest has been paid) = £100 + £2.00 = £102.00

Interest charged at the end of the second month = £102.00 x 2 % = £2.04

Starting balance on the loan at the start of the third month (assuming no interest has been paid) = £102.00 + £2.04 = £104.04

Interest charged at the end of the third month = £104.04 x 2% = £2.08 (rounded to the nearest penny)

Starting balance on the loan at the start of the fourth month (assuming no interest has been paid) = £104.04 + £2.08 = £106.12

Interest charged at the end of the fourth month = £106.12 x 2% = £2.12 (rounded to the nearest penny)

Starting balance on the loan at the start of the fifth month (assuming no interest has been paid) = £106.12 + £2.12 = £108.24

Interest charged at the end of the fifth month = £108.24 x 2% = £2.16 (rounded to the nearest penny)

Starting balance on the loan at the start of the sixth month (assuming no interest has been paid) = £108.24 + £2.16 = £110.40

Interest charged at the end of the sixth month = £110.40 x 2% = £2.21 (rounded to the nearest penny)

Starting balance on the loan at the start of the seventh month (assuming no interest has been paid) = £110.40 + £2.21 = £112.61

Interest charged at the end of the seventh month = £112.61 x 2% = £2.25 (rounded to the nearest penny)

Starting balance on the loan at the start of the eighth month (assuming no interest has been paid) = £112.61 + £2.25 = £114.86

Interest charged at the end of the eighth month = £114.86 x 2% = £2.30 (rounded to the nearest penny)

Starting balance on the loan at the start of the ninth month (assuming no interest has been paid) = £114.86 + £2.30 = £117.16

Interest charged at the end of the ninth month = £117.16 x 2% = £2.34 (rounded to the nearest penny)

Starting balance on the loan at the start of the tenth month (assuming no interest has been paid) = £117.16 + £2.34 = £119.50

Interest charged at the end of the tenth month = £119.50 x 2% = £2.39 (rounded to the nearest penny)

Starting balance on the loan at the start of the eleventh month (assuming no interest has been paid) = £119.50 + £2.39 = £121.89

Interest charged at the end of the eleventh month = £121.89 x 2% = £2.44 (rounded to the nearest penny)

Starting balance on the loan at the start of the twelfth month (assuming no interest has been paid) = £121.89 + £2.44 = £124.33

Interest charged at the end of the twelfth month = £124.33 x 2% = £2.49 (rounded to the nearest penny)

Balance on the loan at the end of the year (assuming no interest has been paid) = £124.33 + £2.49 = £126.82

Step 3: *Use the ending balance on the loan calculated in Step 2, work out the effective interest charged for the year.*

Ending balance less starting balance = £126.82 – £100.00 = £26.82 effective interest charged over the year

Step 4: *Express the effective interest charged as a percentage of the starting balance to give the effective annual rate.*

Effective interest divided by starting balance = £26.82/£100.00 = 0.2682

Multiplied by 100 to give a percentage = 0.2682 x 100 = 26.82%

Exercise 3 – Effective Annual Rate Calculation (Alternative Approach)

Step 1: *Calculate the interest rate charged for each period specified by the loan.*

This is given as 2% per month. It can also be calculated by dividing the annual quoted rate of 24% by 12 (because there are 12 months in each year).

Step 2: *Express the rate from Step 1 as a decimal, by dividing it by 100.*

2/100 is 0.02

Step 3: *Add 1 to the result from Step 2 and multiply it by itself by the number of times interest will be charged over the year.*

1 + 0.02 = 1.02

1.02 multiplied by itself 12 times (since interest is charged monthly = 1.02^{12} = 1.2682

Step 4: *Deduct 1 from the result of Step 3 and express the result as a percentage by multiplying it by 100.*

1.2682 – 1 = 0.2682
0.2682 x 100 = 26.82%

Exercise 4 – The Value of a Bank's Security

The value of the house starts at $250,000 and the bank lends 80% of this value (80% x $250,000 = $200,000).

The house could fall in value by up to $50,000 (20% of the purchase price) and the bank would still be able to get all of its money back by selling it.

However, if the value were to fall below $200,000, the bank's security would not be sufficient to recoup the entire loan.

The bank's security would become zero only if the house were to become worthless.

Exercise 5 – Which Form of Borrowing is Cheapest?

Borrowing source	Ranking (1 = least expensive; 6 = most expensive)	Explanation
Greg is in great need of cash, having exhausted most sources and being unemployed. He manages to find a pawnbroker willing to lend him $2,000, but he has to deposit his wife's wedding ring with the pawnbroker.	5	Owing to the secured nature of pawnbroking, the borrowing costs tend to be cheaper than payday loans, although pawnbrokers are more expensive than most other forms of borrowing since they are attracting the more desperate borrower like Greg.
Aaron is a reasonably well-paid office worker who has saved up enough cash to enable him to pay 10% of the purchase price of a $200,000 flat. The remainder will come from a bank in the form of a mortgage loan.	1	This is likely to be the least expensive form of borrowing. Not only is the loan secured on the flat, but Aaron has also managed to fund 10% of the purchase price, so the loan only represents 90% of the value of the flat it is secured against.
Maya is a trainee solicitor and has just rented her first flat. Unfortunately, the flat is lacking a washing machine and Maya is borrowing $1,000 in the form of an unsecured loan from a bank to enable her to buy a washing machine and have it plumbed in.	2	This source of finance is likely to be cheaper than most due to the structured nature of the loan and the fact that Maya is an aspiring professional and therefore likely to be able to repay and service the loan. However, without any security the loan is likely to be more expensive than a mortgage loan.
Zeenat is 25 years old and is a very capable musician. She is self-employed and tends to be particularly busy in the winter season in theatre orchestras. To cover the seasonal nature of her earnings, she has arranged a $1,500 overdraft facility with her bank.	3	The flexibility required of Zeenat from her overdraft means that it is likely to be more expensive than the unsecured loan from the bank. However, bank finance is generally cheaper than credit cards and other more desperate forms of borrowing from pawnbrokers and payday loan providers.

Borrowing source	Ranking (1 = least expensive; 6 = most expensive)	Explanation
Rajiv is 30 and is trying very hard to establish a business as a DJ. He has a regular slot at a nightspot in his local town, and in order to widen his appeal he is planning to purchase some new equipment that will cost around $1,200. Rajiv decides that the best way to fund the purchase is to buy the equipment on his credit card, which he hopes he will be in a position to repay in full in six months or so.	4	Rajiv will pay substantial interest by not paying off his credit card in full each month. The interest charged is likely to be higher than overdrafts.
Mohammed is employed but has got himself into a financial mess with his love of expensive holidays. He is finding it very difficult to get any more borrowing from his bank or his credit card providers. He has decided to borrow $500 in the form of a payday loan that will cover him until he gets paid in two weeks.	6	Mohammed's borrowing is likely to be more expensive than all of the others. Payday loans represent unsecured loans for the desperate borrower and are priced accordingly by the providers – they are very expensive.

Exercise 6 – The Trivandrum Tigers and Culchester United

In both situations the broad consideration is whether to borrow the money or to sell shares.

The Trivandrum Tigers' requirement is for $50 million to attract the best stars to its team. This is highly speculative – there is no guarantee that attracting big-name stars will translate into success on the pitch. As a result, it may be inappropriate to borrow the money as the Tigers may find it difficult to pay the interest and then repay the borrowed funds. Additional equity finance will probably be most appropriate. By selling shares, if the strategy does not provide the hoped-for success, the Tigers will not be burdened with interest and repayment requirements.

Culchester United's requirement is for £1 billion to construct a new stadium. Culchester United could raise money by selling further shares, but, given that this finance will be used to construct a property, there is a possibility of raising debt. As well as offering some security to the lender, the stadium development should result in increased income from attendance that could be used to pay interest, and renting or selling homes in the residential development should also generate additional cash.

Assuming the debt finance route is chosen, the £1 billion being raised is probably large enough to make a Culchester United bond issue a possibility. This will potentially be cheaper than borrowing from banks since it raises finance directly from investors.

Exercise 7 – Mortgages

7. C (chapter 3, section 2.1).

The substantial amounts of money required to buy property mean borrowing is generally over a long period of time and secured on the property – a mortgage loan.

Exercise 8 – Effective Annual Rate

8. B (chapter 3, section 3.1).

The effective annual rate will be greater than 10% as long as interest is charged more frequently than once per annum. The effective annual rate here is approximately 10.38%, based on the following calculation:

Step 1: 10% divided by 4 quarters = 2.5% per quarter

Step 2: Expressed as a decimal = 0.025

Step 3: Adding 1 and multiplying by itself 4 times = $1.025^4 = 1.1038$

Deducting 1 and expressing as a percentage = 10.38%

Exercise 9 – Effective Annual Rate

9. C (chapter 3, section 3.1).

The effective annual rate is most easily calculated using the following approach:

Step 1: 12% divided by 12 months = 1% per month

Step 2: Expressed as a decimal = 0.01

Step 3: Adding 1 and multiplying by itself 12 times = $1.01^{12} = 1.1268$

Deducting 1 and expressing as a percentage = 12.68%

Exercise 10 – Investment Banks

10. D (chapter 3, section 6).

Investment banks specialise in capital raising and advise on strategy including M&A.

Exercise 11 – Central Banks

11. A (chapter 3, section 7).

The central bank, such as the US Federal Reserve, has three main activities – acting as banker to the government, acting as banker to the banks and regulating the banks.

Fundamentals of Financial Services

Equities

This syllabus area will provide approximately 5 of the 30 examination questions

Equities

This chapter focuses on equities, which are alternatively referred to as shares or stock. Equities were briefly introduced in chapter 2. This chapter will add some further detail as well as reinforce what has already been covered.

1. The Reasons for Issuing Shares

Learning Objective 4.1.1

Know the reasons for issuing shares (stock) – to finance a company

A fictional example was introduced in chapter 2 regarding a start-up company called CareerComic.

⚙ Example

Two young college graduates have a great idea. They think that other college graduates and schoolchildren would love to have access to a database of available careers that are portrayed in a fun, simple and understandable way that would appeal. They want to pull together a comic strip of a day in the life of each career – CareerComic.

They have talked to people about their plans for CareerComic and they have potentially found someone who will provide them with some money to get a prototype established. That person is willing to provide money in return for a stake in the business. They are hoping the business might grow and be worth a lot of money one day.

Companies like CareerComic cost money to set up – even if the founding graduates are willing to provide their time at no cost, the company will still incur costs such as renting office space from which to operate, the bills for electricity and water that will come with the offices, plus the cost of equipment (such as computers, printers, or phones) and possibly advertising and marketing the product.

The long-term finance for this capital that is required by start-up companies can come from borrowing, selling equity or a combination of both.

In our CareerComic example, the founders decided to sell equity. Every company issues equity and it is the owners of equity that own the company. Below is a bit more detail about the equity in CareerComic.

⚙ Example

CareerComic is incorporated as a company – strictly it is CareerComic inc – and the original owners of the company were the two brains behind the idea: Brad Michaels and Marvin Gardner. Brad and Marvin each put $50 into the company and were given 50 shares. As the CareerComic idea was developed further, Brad and Marvin got talking to Warren, a local businessman. Warren liked the idea and wanted to invest in it. Warren agreed to pay $3,000 for another 100 shares in CareerComic Inc.

CareerComic's shares in issue have increased. Since Brad and Marvin originally held 100 shares, and Warren has purchased a further 100, CareerComic now has 200 shares in issue. With 200 shares in issue, Warren has the most shares. He holds 100, so he has half of the company, or 50%. Brad and Marvin each own 50 shares, so they each own a quarter (25%) of the company.

The reason for CareerComic selling more shares to Warren was to raise more finance. The additional $3,000 from Warren will be enough to finance CareerComic into its next stage, building up its product and starting to market it to potential customers.

A further benefit of involving Warren may be that, as an established businessman, his contacts and know-how will be very useful too.

In the CareerComic example, the price Brad and Marvin paid for their shares was just $1 each, and later on Warren agreed to pay $30 for each of his shares. Brad and Marvin demanded more than $1 per share and Warren was willing to pay more because he was buying a part of their idea. The concept of CareerComic came from Brad and Marvin and they spent their time coming up with it and establishing CareerComic inc. Warren was investing in something that was already established. It was Warren's view that Brad and Marvin's concept of CareerComic was a good one, and for him to become involved he had to recognise the value of that idea by paying more than the $1 that Brad and Marvin paid for their shares.

In summary, as illustrated by the CareerComic example, the major reason for a company issuing shares is to raise finance.

Exercise 1 – Fuelmonitor ltd

Fuelmonitor ltd is a company that has been recently set up to provide details of the cheapest car fuel prices in the subscribers' local area by email each week. Fuelmonitor hopes to generate revenues both from subscription and from site sponsorship. Fuelmonitor was set up by Patrick Brightman, who paid £300 for all 30 shares that Fuelmonitor issued.

During the first months of its existence, Patrick has set up a website for Fuelmonitor and researched fuel prices in his local area. Fuelmonitor has attracted some subscribers and has a local newspaper interested in sponsoring the site. It now needs more finance to expand and is planning to issue new equity. Patrick has a list of contacts that he feels may be interested in buying the 20 new shares Fuelmonitor will issue.

1. *How much should Fuelmonitor issue the new shares for? £10, less than £10 or more than £10?*

2. After issuing the new shares, what will Patrick's ownership proportion of Fuelmonitor be?
3. What will be the proportion of Fuelmonitor owned by the new shareholders?
4. How might the shareholders of Fuelmonitor get a return on their investment?

The answers to the exercise can be found in the appendix at the end of the chapter.

2. Initial Public Offerings (IPOs)

Learning Objective 4.1.2
Know the definition of an initial public offering (IPO)

As the name suggests, an initial public offering (IPO) is the first time shares are offered to members of the public.

In the CareerComic example we have just looked at, an IPO has not happened with the sale of shares to Warren because he is just one selected person. An IPO is a general offer that is made widely available by offering the shares to unconnected third parties. CareerComic might see an IPO as the ultimate aim for the company, as detailed below.

⚙ Example

Let's assume that CareerComic has now been established for a number of years since Warren's investment. Both Warren's business know-how and the popularity of the product have made CareerComic very successful. It is generating a healthy profit, and has paid dividends to its shareholders for the last two years. It now has international appeal and, as well as being very successful in the US, it is being heavily used in Asia.

Warren, Brad and Marvin decide that CareerComic needs to raise further money that will enable it to continue its global expansion, in particular the creation of a Mandarin version for the Chinese market.

CareerComic inc decides that it will offer new shares to the public in an IPO. Not only will the IPO enable CareerComic to raise money, but the publicity surrounding it will increase awareness of the product too.

As mentioned in chapter 2, a pertinent example of an IPO was Alibaba, which came a couple of years after the IPO of the social networking site, Facebook.

⚙ Example

The Facebook IPO

Facebook sold more than 400 million shares at $38 per share in May 2012, raising almost $7 billion for the company and allowing some earlier investors to sell their shares at a substantial profit.

As well as the early investors, the founder and CEO Mark Zuckerberg sold some of his shares in the IPO, receiving more than $1 billion. However, six months after the IPO, the investors were not doing so well, with the Facebook share price falling to about half of the $38 IPO price. Since then, the shares have recovered and, in January 2019, they were trading at $149, nearly four times their initial sale price.

A key part of an IPO is that the issuing company will have its shares subsequently traded on a stock exchange. After all, the public that buy shares in an IPO will want the ability to sell those shares at a later date. When a company's shares begin trading on a stock exchange, the company is often described as becoming listed. Facebook is listed on the **NASDAQ,** the US stock exchange that specialises in technology company shares.

Like Alibaba and Facebook, Google also sold shares to the public, although this happened in 2004.

> ⚙️ **Example**

The Google IPO

It was 2004 when Google became a listed company. Like Facebook, Google chose to list on NASDAQ, and Google sold around 19.5 million shares at $85 each to raise approximately $1.7 billion. Most of the money raised went to the company. On the first day of trading, Google shares rose to $100. After a change of name for the company that owns the Google search engine to Alphabet in October 2015, the shares were changing hands for over $1,000 each in January 2019. The investors who purchased Google shares in the IPO have done rather well.

In summary, an initial public offering is:

- commonly referred to as an IPO
- when a company first makes its shares available to the public
- when the company becomes listed on a stock exchange.

See also chapter 6, section 2.

3. Potential Returns from Shares

Learning Objective 4.1.3
Know the potential sources of return from shares: dividend; capital gain

Learning Objective 4.1.4
Be able to calculate the dividend yield given the share price and the dividends paid in the year

---

An investor buying shares is hoping for a combination of two things to provide a return – dividends and a **capital gain**.

Dividends are the regular ongoing income that a shareholder may receive. Many well-established listed companies pay dividends every quarter or every half-year. The amount of dividend paid is not fixed; instead it is determined by the management of the company and driven mainly by two things – profitability and expectation.

This is illustrated in the fictional example that follows:

> ⚙️ **Example**

ABM inc is a well-established manufacturer of sophisticated computer equipment. It is listed on the New York Stock Exchange (NYSE) and has shown a pattern of increasing its quarterly dividends by around 10% each year for the last three years. In the same quarter of the previous year, ABM paid a 90 cents dividend on each share.

This quarter has been a good one. After winning some significant new business, profits are up 15% on a year earlier. ABM's management decides that it is right to increase the quarterly dividend by 10% to 99 cents per share. The dividend increase should meet the expectation of the shareholders, since it continues the established pattern, and it is comfortably covered by the percentage increase in company profits.

Dividends are usually expressed both in absolute terms, such as 99 cents in the previous example, and as a percentage of the share price. When expressed as a percentage of the share price, the resultant figure is described as the **dividend yield**. A bigger dividend yield means a greater proportion of the share price is being paid to investors. So if the investor is looking to generate income from their investment, then a bigger dividend yield is better than a smaller dividend yield.

> ⚙️ **Example**

ABM inc paid dividends of 99 cents per share in each of the last four quarters – a total of $3.96 for the year. If the ABM share price is currently $150, then the dividend yield is (3.96/150) x 100 = 2.64%.

Exercise 2 – Dividend Yield

Below are details for three fictional companies. What is the dividend yield for each?

Company name	Total dividends paid in the last year ($)	Share price ($)	Dividend yield (%)
ABC inc	4.32	172.00	
FGH inc	8.64	403.00	
XYZ inc	12.24	702.00	

The answer to this exercise can be found in the appendix at the end of this chapter.

Equity investors hope their shares will increase in value – make a capital gain – as well as pay regular income in the form of dividends. As we have already seen, many larger company shares are regularly traded on stock exchanges. The stock exchanges provide information about the prices at which shares are currently trading, so assessing the extent to which listed shares are gaining in value is straightforward. This is illustrated by continuing with the ABM inc example below.

⚙ Example

James Lester holds a significant number of shares in ABM inc. He purchased the shares at an average price of $100 some years ago, and just prior to the announcement of the latest quarterly results, the ABM share price was $150. Obviously, James is pleased to see that the latest quarterly results from ABM are strong and even happier to see that, as a result, the trading price of ABM shares increases to $165.

James decides that he will sell a significant number of his shares, realising a capital gain of $65 per share ($165 – $100).

Before the announcement of the quarterly results, James's position was pretty good – he was already 50% up, although he had not actually sold any shares at that point. However, when the share price increased to $165, the 65% gain was enough to prompt him to sell at least some of his shares.

As shown in the examples above, shares have the potential to provide returns to the investor in two ways, by:

- paying regular dividends
- increasing in value to deliver a capital gain.

However, it is important to point out that investments in equity do not always go the way of ABM inc in the previous example. Unprofitable companies may be unable to afford to pay dividends, so the shareholders will not get any income. Furthermore, the price of shares can go down – so investors can end up facing capital losses rather than capital gains. In summary:

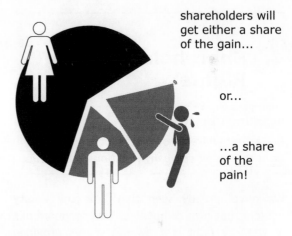

shareholders will get either a share of the gain...

or...

...a share of the pain!

Exercise 3 – Which Share Offers the Best Investment Opportunity?

The January 2019 details in relation to the shares of six well-established US listed companies (Apple, Exxon Mobil, Alphabet, JPMorgan Chase, McDonald's and Microsoft®) are provided below.

You may already be familiar with these companies, but if not, then please do a little research on them and try answering the following questions for each:

- *What does the company do?*
- *What products does the company sell?*
- *Do you use the company's products? If not, do you know people who do and do you anticipate using them in the next few years?*

Then combine your research with the details in the table about each company's shares and

Company name	Current share price ($)	Share price high in the last year ($)	Share price low in the last year ($)	Dividend yield (%)
Apple	154.60	233.47	142.00	1.95
Exxon Mobil	71.75	89.30	64.65	4.55
Alphabet	1,085.44	1,273.89	970.11	0.00
JPMorgan Chase	102.49	119.33	91.11	3.19
McDonald's	180.97	190.88	146.84	2.56
Microsoft®	105.68	116.18	83.83	1.78

determine which share do you think offers the best value as an investment and why.

A suggested answer is provided in the appendix to this chapter.

The Owners of the Company (the Shareholders)

Decisions made by vote

Information about performance

The Management of the Company (the Executives)

4. Shareholder Voting Rights

Learning Objective 4.1.5

Know that shares provide their owners with the right to vote at company meetings/assemblies

We have already seen that it is the equity holders that own companies. This section looks at the key right that owning shares provides – the right to attend and vote at company meetings.

In different parts of the world, company meetings are referred to in different ways. They are often referred to as company assemblies, or even general assemblies. Typically, they occur once a year and, however they are termed, the format and purpose is the same – these meetings give the owners of the company (the shareholders) the opportunity to find out how the company is performing and to make decisions on what should happen.

The reason that company meetings are necessary is simple. It is very often the case that the day-to-day management of a company is performed by persons who are not the owners of that company, as shown below.

As the above diagram shows, it is at company meetings that the management of the company (the executives including the chief executive) provide an update for the owners (the shareholders) and are also available to be questioned about the company's performance and plans. The owners can then make decisions on a variety of matters, such as the salary paid to the chief executive. These decisions are voted on, and in most cases they are agreed when the majority vote in favour.

⚙ Example

Joseph is a shareholder in a large listed bank, VBS Bank inc. VBS's annual company meeting is scheduled to happen in a month's time and Joseph receives an invitation to attend with some financial information about VBS's recent performance that includes a proposed salary increase for VBS's executive directors. Joseph can go along to the meeting and will have the opportunity to vote on significant matters, including whether he feels the executive directors' pay increases are justified and should go ahead.

However, even if Joseph votes against the increases, it may not prevent the pay awards going ahead. The decision will be made on a simple majority of the voting shareholders.

As shown above, it is the shareholders, as owners of the business, who need to be made aware of how the company is performing and who make key decisions, such as whether the pay levels for the company's executive directors are excessive. In summary, company meetings or assemblies:

- are meetings to which all of the shareholders are invited
- are generally required to be held at least annually
- provide the opportunity for the owners of the company (the shareholders) to vote on significant matters.

5. The Risks Involved in Owning Shares

Learning Objective 4.1.6

Know the risks involved in owning shares: lack of profit; bankruptcy/collapse

As owners of a company, the shareholders face the risk that the company does not do well. If the company makes no profit, it will not be in a position to pay any dividends to the shareholders and those shareholders are unlikely to be able to sell their shares and make any capital gain.

In the extreme case, if a company collapses into **bankruptcy** the shareholders will get nothing, as shown in the following illustration:

⚙ Example

Tom Clarke thinks he has found a way to manufacture the ultimate yo-yo using recycled tin cans. He is confident that the combination of the popularity of yo-yos with the environmentally friendly use of recycled materials will make his yo-yos a big success.

He sets up a company – Yo-Yo ltd – to manufacture and sell the yo-yos, selling some shares to his friend Max and using some of his own money to buy the remainder. Max contributes £10,000 and Tom contributes £5,000, so Yo-Yo ltd starts with £15,000 of cash, as shown below:

	Total
Max buys 1,000 shares for £10 each	£10,000
Tom buys 1,000 shares for £5 each	£5,000
Yo-Yo ltd starting cash	£15,000

Unfortunately, the business does not do well. After struggling for a couple of years, the company runs out of cash. Since it still owes a few hundred dollars in rent, the company is declared bankrupt and unable to pay its bills.

Tom and Max have lost their £15,000 and the only bit of good news for Tom and his co-investor friend is that they cannot lose any more than their invested money. As shareholders they are legally separate from the company – their shares are worth nothing, but they do not have to pay the company's bills.

So, who does pay the unpaid bills? The answer is no-one – the landlord will not get the unpaid rent.

Equity is at the bottom of the food chain.

- In the event of collapse it will be the lenders that get their money first.
- Only if anything is left will the shareholders get anything at all.

In summary, the risks faced by shareholders are:

- that the company's level of profits (or losses) means it is unable to pay dividends
- that the value of shares falls – potentially to zero if the company collapses into bankruptcy.

Exercise 4

All of the following are potential sources of return from shares EXCEPT?

a.   Regular dividends
b.   Capital gain
c.   Increasing dividends
d.   Coupons

Exercise 5

An unsuccessful company collapses and falls into bankruptcy. Which of the following best describes what will happen to the unpaid debts?

a.   The company's bankers will pay them
b.   The company's shareholders will pay them
c.   They will be paid by the government
d.   They will remain unpaid

⚙️ Answers to Chapter Exercises

Exercise 1 – Fuelmonitor ltd

Fuelmonitor was set up by Patrick Brightman who paid £300 for all 30 shares that Fuelmonitor issued. After setting up its website, Fuelmonitor has attracted some subscribers and has a local newspaper interested in sponsoring the site. It now needs more finance to expand and is planning to issue 20 new shares.

1) How much should Fuelmonitor issue the new shares for?

Given that Fuelmonitor has already set up a website and started to attract interest and some business, it is logical to expect its shares to have a value in excess of the original £10 Patrick paid. Precisely how much would be judged by the existing and potential profitability of Fuelmonitor ltd.

2) After issuing the new shares, what will Patrick's ownership proportion of Fuelmonitor be?

Patrick originally held all 30 shares that Fuelmonitor had issued. Now the addition of 20 new shares means that Patrick owns 30 of the 50 shares in issue – 60% of the company.

3) What will be the proportion of Fuelmonitor owned by the new shareholders?

The new shareholders will hold 20 of the 50 shares in issue, which represents 40% of the company.

4) How will the shareholders of Fuelmonitor get a return on their investment?

The shareholders of Fuelmonitor will hope that the company will make enough profits to pay them regular dividends and they will also hope that Fuelmonitor will become more valuable so they can sell the shares for more than they paid for them.

Exercise 2 – Dividend Yield

Below are details relating to three fictional companies. What is the dividend yield for each?

Company name	Total dividends paid in the last year ($)	Share price ($)	Dividend yield (%)
ABC inc	4.32	172.00	2.51%
FGH inc	8.64	403.00	2.14%
XYZ inc	12.24	702.00	1.74%

Exercise 3 – Which Share Offers the Best Investment Opportunity?

Company name	Current share price ($)	Share price high in the last year ($)	Share price low in the last year ($)	Dividend yield (%)
Apple	154.60	233.47	142.00	1.95
Exxon Mobil	71.75	89.30	64.65	4.55
Alphabet	1,085.44	1,273.89	970.11	0.00
JPMorgan Chase	102.49	119.33	91.11	3.19
McDonald's	180.97	190.88	146.84	2.56
Microsoft®	105.68	116.18	83.83	1.78

Deciding which share offers the best value as an investment and why is no easy task, and there is no one right answer. It is very much a matter of judgement.

However, looking at each column in turn and considering which company might be best is a logical way of approaching the task. The overall picture after considering each column will hopefully reveal which one may be the best investment opportunity.

The first column provides only the company name, and your research about what these companies do and what products they sell may help you determine which ones are better investment opportunities than others.

- **Apple** is known to be an extremely successful company with products like the iPad, and iPhone that are increasingly sophisticated and considered as 'must haves' by many consumers.
- **Exxon Mobil** is one of the world's biggest oil companies, and oil, plus the products extracted from it, are vital to run motor vehicles, ships and aeroplanes; and provide energy.
- **Alphabet is the owner of Google** – the way most people find what they are looking for on the internet, and the company is very effective at selling targeted advertising that reaches people who are likely to be interested in the products being offered.
- **JPMorgan Chase** is one of the world's largest banks. It does everything including retail, corporate and investment banking.
- **McDonald's** is the most well-known fast-food brand in the world, selling meals to millions every day from almost every city on the planet.
- **Microsoft**® provides the software that most computers around the world rely on, particularly those used for business purposes.

The second column provides the share prices. Alone, these are not particularly useful. Although Exxon Mobil shares are the least expensive to purchase and far cheaper than Alphabet in particular, this is not helpful from an investment perspective. Each company will have different numbers of shares in issue, so some are essentially bigger slices of the whole than others.

When the current share price in column two is combined with the highs and lows from the last year (columns three and four), more investment insight can be gathered. McDonald's is the closest to its annual high point, suggesting it is perhaps not the right time to buy as there may not be a lot of scope for the price to increase in the short term. In contrast, Apple is quite close to its low for the year, which may indicate a bargain at the current price or concern for its future. For example, one of the reasons for Apple's share price being so close to its low point is that iPhone sales growth is slowing, particularly in China – if investors think this is temporary and that new models will reinvigorate sales growth, this might be a good time to buy but if investors think this is the beginning of a long-term decline, they may decide to sell.

The final column gives the dividend yield as a percentage. Generally, a high dividend yield is more attractive as it indicates a strong level of income will be forthcoming. Exxon Mobil, JPMorgan Chase and McDonald's are three well-established, profit-making businesses and are paying 4.55%, 3.19% and 2.56% respectively, while Apple, which previously paid a tiny dividend, now has sufficient cash to pay a more respectable dividend yield of 1.95%.

Ultimately it is a question of judgement. For investors looking for income and possible growth in the short term, perhaps Apple is the best with a dividend yield of 1.95% and a share price near the year's low point.

However, please be aware that this is only superficial analysis. Many would say that the other two technology companies such as Alphabet with its innovative portfolio and the more established Microsoft® have a greater potential to grow, and there are investment cases to be made for the others too. These include Exxon Mobil's substantial oil reserves, JPMorgan Chase's huge presence and customer base; and McDonald's, which has established, well-known products which are now a part of the eating culture in many countries.

Exercise 4 – Potential Sources of Return

4. D (chapter 4, section 3).

The potential sources of return on shares are dividends and capital gains. Coupons are paid by bonds, not shares.

Exercise 5 - Bankruptcy

5. D (chapter 4, section 5)

Shareholders are separate to the company, so if a company collapses, some of its debts may remain unpaid but the shares will be worthless.

Fundamentals of Financial Services

Bonds

5

1. **Introduction to Bonds** — 63
2. **Bond Issuers** — 64
3. **Features of Bonds** — 65
4. **Bond Terminology** — 66
5. **Advantages and Disadvantages of Investing in Bonds** — 68
6. **Credit Rating Agencies** — 70
7. **Bonds or Equities?** — 71

This syllabus area will provide approximately 6 of the 30 examination questions

Fundamentals of Financial Services

Bonds

1. Introduction to Bonds

Learning Objective 5.1.1

Know the definition of a bond and the reasons for issue: alternative to loans or issuing shares

Having already encountered bonds earlier in this workbook, we know bonds are essentially IOUs. However, a more formal definition of a bond would be: a debt instrument whereby an investor lends money to an entity (such as a company or a government) that borrows the funds for a defined period of time at a fixed interest rate.

Clearly, the reason for issuing bonds is for the issuer to raise finance, perhaps to fund something in particular as shown in the example below.

⚙ Example

Crazy Jet inc is a small airline that has been successful to date and wants to expand its fleet of aircraft. Needing to raise the necessary cash from somewhere, Crazy Jet considers borrowing the money from a bank, and is quoted an interest rate of 8% for the five-year loan it is looking for. Instead, it decides to issue 1,000 bonds, each for $1,000, in order to raise the finance to buy more aircraft. Crazy Jet will pay just 5% interest on the bonds.

Will Lend has $1,000 to invest. He has travelled on Crazy Jet and particularly enjoyed the experience. He decides to buy a bond, paying $1,000 and receiving the following:

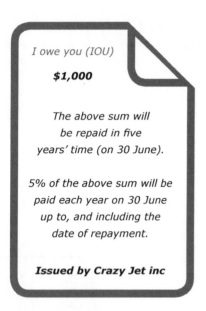

> I owe you (IOU)
>
> **$1,000**
>
> *The above sum will
> be repaid in five
> years' time (on 30 June).*
>
> *5% of the above sum will be
> paid each year on 30 June
> up to, and including the
> date of repayment.*
>
> **Issued by Crazy Jet inc**

As shown in the above example, the issuer of the bonds (Crazy Jet) chose to issue bonds in preference to other potential forms of finance. The bonds were actually cheaper (costing 5% in interest) than the bank loan that was available (costing 8% in interest).

Exercise 1 – Crazy Jet's Financing

Why do you think Crazy Jet might not have wanted to issue equity as an alternative to borrowing the money?

The answer to this exercise can be found in the appendix at the end of the chapter.

So, bonds are one of three major ways for a company to raise finance. The alternatives are bank loans and equity issues.

2. Bond Issuers

Learning Objective 5.1.2

Know the bond issuers: governments; corporates

The issuers of bonds can be subdivided into two major groups – companies and governments.

The Two Major Issuers of Bonds

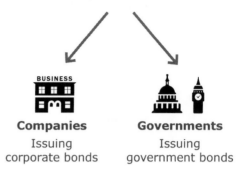

Companies	Governments
Issuing corporate bonds	Issuing government bonds

Since companies are alternatively referred to as corporates, bonds issued by companies are often termed 'corporate bonds'.

⚙ Example

Microsoft® Bond Issue, August 2016

Microsoft®, the world's largest software maker, sold $19.75 billion of corporate bonds in August 2016. It chose to sell seven individual groups of bonds, repaying the money at different dates and paying different interest rates as follows:

Quantity issued	Repayment	Interest payment
$2.5bn	3 years	1.1% pa
$2.75bn	5 years	1.55% pa
$1.5bn	7 years	2.0% pa
$4.0bn	10 years	2.4%
$2.25bn	20 years	3.45%
$4.5bn	30 years	3.7%
$2.25bn	40 years	3.95%
Total $19.75bn		

Microsoft® was unspecific about how the money raised will be used although some of the proceeds were probably used to help fund the previously announced acquisition of LinkedIn Corp for $26.2 billion in cash. The different interest rates payable on the seven bonds are driven by the returns demanded by investors for bonds with different repayment dates.

The fact that the required interest payment increases as the time to repayment increases is a function of risk and reward. Longer-dated bonds are more risky and hence the investors

want greater returns – Microsoft® is more likely to have problems over the next 40 years than over the next three years.

As the above example shows, companies can choose to issue bonds with different dates of repayment. The repayment dates chosen will depend on a number of factors, including the financial plans of the issuing company and the periods over which investors may wish to invest.

A significant number of developed countries' governments issue bonds, as they often spend more in a given year than they receive in taxes. Major countries like the US, Germany, France and the UK are all significant issuers of government bonds.

⚙ Example

UK Government Bond Issue, January 2019

The UK government sold £2.25 billion of bonds called **Treasury** Gilts in January 2019. The bonds will repay the borrowed money in 2028 and will pay interest of 1.625% each year.

Exercise 2 – Government Bonds

Why do governments such as the US and the UK issue bonds?

The answer to this exercise can be found in the appendix at the end of the chapter.

To provide some insight into the reasons governments might want to borrow, the following example outlines the US federal budget for the year ending 30 September 2019. The federal budget is the expected income and expenditure of the US for the period and shows that expenditure exceeds income.

This deficit needs to be funded in some way and increases the US's national debt.

⚙ Example

US Federal Budget 2019

Total expected receipts, mainly from taxes, add up to $3.422 trillion. Total expenditure adds up to approximately $4.407 trillion.

The difference between the two is that the expected spending is approximately $0.985 trillion (that is 985 thousand million dollars!) more than the receipts. This difference will need to be funded through the issue of US Treasury bonds.

3. Features of Bonds

Learning Objective 5.1.3

Know the features of bonds: repayment date; frequency of interest payments; tradeable

All bonds tend to exhibit certain key features – particularly a date when the bond will repay the money loaned and the frequency at which the interest payments will be made. Returning to our earlier example of the Crazy Jet corporate bond, both of these features are clearly displayed:

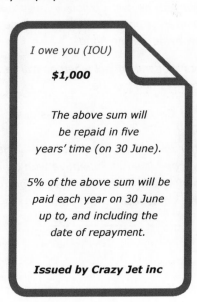

I owe you (IOU)

$1,000

The above sum will be repaid in five years' time (on 30 June).

5% of the above sum will be paid each year on 30 June up to, and including the date of repayment.

Issued by Crazy Jet inc

The repayment date is in five years' time and the interest payments are paid annually on 30 June. Each interest payment will be 5% x $1,000 = $50. Some bonds pay interest more frequently, perhaps semi-annually rather than annually. If the Crazy Jet bond paid interest semi-annually then it would split the annual $50 into two $25 payments, one on 31 December and the other on 30 June.

Bonds are tradeable instruments. This means that they can be bought and sold. To see why this feature might be important, let's revisit Will Lend, who purchased a Crazy Jet bond in the earlier example.

⚙ Example

You will recall that Will Lend purchased a Crazy Jet bond that will repay $1,000 in five years' time and pays annual interest of 5%, or $50 every year on 30 June.

Three years have elapsed and Will has money problems himself. He is trying to get together enough cash to buy a car and could really benefit from an additional $1,000. The answer may lie with the Crazy Jet bond – the bonds can be traded, so Will can offer the bond for sale. Hopefully, he will be able to get $1,000 for the bond two years earlier than the repayment date. However, he will obviously miss out on any more interest payments – these will be paid to the new owner of the bond.

The factors that will impact whether Will can get $1,000 for his bond include:

1. *whether Crazy Jet is still successful in business*
2. *whether the 5% coupon that is available on the bond is still competitive with other forms of investments, such as the interest payable on deposits with banks.*

Bond Features

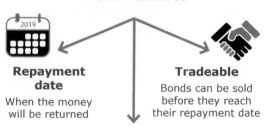

Repayment date
When the money will be returned

Tradeable
Bonds can be sold before they reach their repayment date

Interest rate and frequency
Percentage paid as interest and how often it is paid

4. Bond Terminology

Learning Objective 5.1.4
Know the key terms: nominal; coupon; redemption/maturity; yield

Like finance generally, there are a number of terms that are used for bonds which need to be understood.

The **nominal value** of a bond is the amount that is owed by the bond issuer, and that will be repaid on the repayment date. It is also referred to as the par value, or as the **face value** (because it is the amount that is written on the face of the bond certificate – the IOU).

The repayment date is usually referred to as the **redemption date**, or the **maturity** date. So commentators will talk about bonds redeeming in perhaps five years' time, or maturing in five years' time.

The interest rate that is applied to the nominal value is more typically termed the **coupon** on the bond.

So, returning to our earlier example of the Crazy Jet bond, we can see that the nominal value or face value is $1,000, the maturity or redemption date is in five years, and the coupon is 5% paid annually on 30 June.

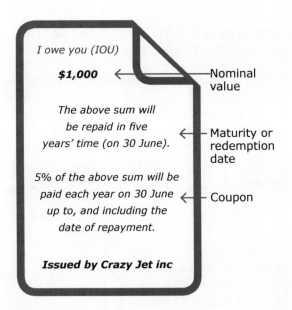

Nominal value

Maturity or redemption date

Coupon

4.1 Bond Yields

The final piece of terminology to consider in relation to bonds is the yield. Yield is another word for return and it is expressed as an annual percentage. For bonds, it is tempting to think that the return – the yield – is the same as the coupon. This is only the case if the bond is being bought and sold at its nominal value. If the traded price rises above or falls below the nominal value, the yield will be different from the coupon, because to calculate the yield you divide the annual coupon by the price paid.

⚙ Example

Returning to the Crazy Jet bond, we saw that when it was issued it was sold at its nominal value of $1,000. So the original buyer, Will Lend, has invested in a bond that will provide him with a yield of 5% – the coupon rate and the yield for the investor are the same, at 5% each year (50/1,000 = 0.05 x 100 = 5%).

Now let's presume that one year has elapsed and the Crazy Jet bonds have four years left to run until they mature. The general economy is going well and interest rates in general have gone up, so alternatives to the Crazy Jet bond, like deposit accounts and other bonds, are offering higher rates of interest of 7%. If Will Lend were to consider selling his bond at this point, no one would be willing to pay $1,000

and only receive 5% yield – they would want a higher yield because higher rates are on offer elsewhere. The required yield has increased, meaning the price of the Crazy Jet bond will fall such that the yield it provides the buyer is competitive.

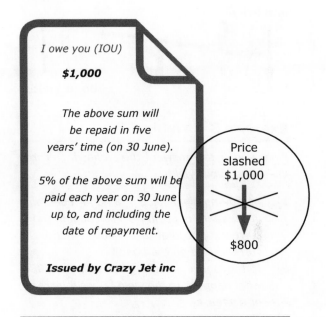

The example above shows that, if interest rates generally increase after a bond issue, then to sell the bond the yield will have to increase to attract any buyer. The only way this can happen is by reducing the price. In the Crazy Jet example, the coupon payment does not change, but the price fall means that the coupon received of $50 is a bigger percentage of the amount paid (6.25%, based on (50/800) x 100).

It would be the opposite situation if interest rates in general fell. Buyers of the bond would be willing to accept a lower yield and the price of the bond would increase.

Note that, if the buyer keeps the bond until its maturity date, the yield will also be supplemented by the fact that the buyer will make a gain when the bond matures and repays $1,000, because they only paid $800 for it. When the yield calculation includes only the calculation of coupon divided by price, it is called the flat yield. When the calculation includes the capital gain (or loss) if the bond is held until its maturity date, it is called the yield to maturity.

In summary, there is an inverse relationship between yield and bond prices. If required yields increase, bond prices decrease; if required yields decrease, bond prices increase. The relationship can be thought of as a see-saw.

Bond Price

Bond Yields

Exercise 3 – Yields

Please try to answer the following three questions about yields:

1) *$1,000 nominal value of a bond redeeming in 30 years is paying a 7% coupon and is currently priced at face value. What is the current yield on the bond?*

2) *If the above bond's price falls to $980, what happens to the yield? Does it increase or decrease?*

3) *If the bond's price now increases to $1,100, what happens to the yield? Does it increase or decrease?*

The answers to this exercise can be found in the appendix at the end of the chapter.

4.2 Interest Rates and Bond Prices

As explained in section 4.1, bond prices are susceptible to movements in general interest rates because for their yield to be attractive to an investor it needs to remain competitive with the return available on alternative investments.

The following exercise explores this further:

Exercise 4 – What Happens to the Bond Price? Part 1

Now you know the relationship between a bond's price and its yield, try to fill in the following table. Are the bonds likely to go up in value, down in value, or stay the same in the following situations?

Situation	Price will go up, down, or stay the same?
The European Central Bank decreases interest rates in the eurozone. What is likely to happen to the bond prices of German and French government bonds?	
The central bank in the UK (the Bank of England) increases interest rates. What will happen to the price of UK government bonds?	

Suggested answers can be found in the appendix at the end of this chapter.

5. Advantages and Disadvantages of Investing in Bonds

Learning Objective 5.1.5

Know the advantages and disadvantages of investing in bonds: regular income; fixed maturity date; credit risk

Now the features and characteristics of bonds have been encountered, the advantages and disadvantages of investing in bonds can be considered. Two particular features provide the key advantages of investing in bonds – coupons and the redemption date.

For investors, a predictable income is seen as an advantage and most bonds pay a stated amount of income every year or half-year in the form of coupons. This is in stark contrast to equities, where the amount of the dividend can be unpredictable as companies have profitable or unprofitable years.

Similarly, it is seen as a positive feature that bonds will repay a set amount of cash at an agreed date in the future. The investors know, when investing, how much and when the redemption will occur. Again this contrasts with investing in equities, where the price at which the shares can be sold is unknown – share prices can go down as well as up.

The potential disadvantage of investing in bonds is the possibility that the issuer will fail to pay some or all of the coupons and the redemption amount because it does not have the available funds. In such circumstances, the issuer is described as being in **default**. Less substantial issuers are more likely to default than other, more substantial issuers. However, rather than a complete default, just an increased possibility of default can have an adverse impact on the return for an investor. This will be the case if the investor has to sell the bond before it reaches maturity. This is illustrated below:

⚙ Example

Carlton Barratt is a musician who has fallen on hard times. Fortunately, when he was earning substantial money he purchased a $10,000 face value 15-year bond paying a 6% annual coupon, issued by Worldwide Resources inc.

The bond's maturity is still seven years away, but Carlton really needs cash now. He decides that selling the bond is the sensible thing to do.

Interest rates remain the same as when he purchased the bond. However, Worldwide Resources has itself not performed well and there is an increased risk that it will default on its bonds. Because of this increase in risk, investors are now looking for an increased return and a yield nearer 14% on Worldwide Resources bonds. This has meant that the resale value of Carlton's bond is only $6,500, compared to the $10,000 that Carlton paid when he purchased the bond.

This example illustrates what happens when a bond is sold before maturity and the risk that the issuer will default has increased. This is alternatively described as an increase in the **credit risk** of the issuer – the risk that the amount owing (the credit) may not be repaid.

Here is a summary of the key advantages of investing in bonds:

- Predictable income in the form of regular, fixed coupons.
- Fixed date and amount to be repaid at redemption.

Here are the key disadvantages of investing in bonds:

- Actual default – the failure of the issuer to be able to pay the coupons and/or the redemption amount.
- An increased risk of default resulting in a fall in the bond's value.

Exercise 5 – What Happens to the Bond Price? Part 2

Try to fill in the following table. Are the bonds likely to go up in value, down in value, or stay the same?

Situation	Price will go up, down, or stay the same?
Buddy inc is an oil exploration company that has just announced a significant discovery of easily accessible oil. What happens to the price of Buddy's 5% coupon-paying bonds?	
Anemone plc's sales have suffered due to a recession in its main market. Anemone has a number of 7% coupon-paying bonds in issue – what is likely to happen to their price?	

Lakeground inc announces a substantial equity issue aimed at reducing its debt burden. What is likely to happen to the price of Lakeground's bonds?	

Suggested answers to this exercise can be found in the appendix at the end of this chapter.

Standard & Poor's/Fitch Ratings	Moody's Ratings
AAA	Aaa
AA	Aa
A	A
BBB	Baa
BB	Ba
B	B
CCC	Caa
CC	Ca
C	C
D	

Increasing levels of credit risk

6. Credit Rating Agencies

Learning Objective 5.1.6

Know the role of credit rating agencies: investment grade/non-investment grade

We have just seen what happens when the credit risk of the issuer of a bond increases – investors become more nervous about whether the coupons will continue to be paid and whether the repayment will happen at maturity. The combination of these two factors means that any new investors are not willing to pay as much for the bond as previously. As what happened with Worldwide Resources bonds, the result is that the bond's price will fall.

Assessing the credit risk for particular bond issues and monitoring any changes is not just done by the existing and potential investors – there are a small number of specialist firms known as credit rating agencies that look at bond issuers and assess the credit risk. There are three dominant **credit rating** agencies globally – Moody's, Standard & Poor's and Fitch Ratings.

All three adopt similar methods for assessing credit risk and have come up with a similar output – an alphabetic system where the safest issuers with least credit risk are termed 'triple A'. Standard & Poor's and Fitch use an identical scale, while the scale adopted by Moody's is slightly different as shown in the next column.

Issuers rated triple A by Standard & Poor's are described as having an '*extremely high capacity to meet their financial commitments*' and by Fitch Ratings as having an '*exceptionally strong capacity for payment of financial commitments*' – in other words, they are likely to be able to pay the bonds' coupons and repay the nominal value at maturity. Moody's describes Aaa as reflecting issuers of the '*highest quality with minimal credit risk*', essentially saying the same thing as the two other agencies. As the credit risk of the issuer increases, the assessment from the agencies moves down the scale with the lowest for Standard & Poor's and Fitch Ratings being D. This is generally for issuers already in default and failing to pay the bond coupons. The lowest rating from Moody's is C.

There is an important dividing line between bonds that are rated by the agencies as having less credit risk, and therefore more appropriate for prudent investors, and bonds that are more risky and therefore less appropriate for prudent investors. This is the dividing line between what are termed investment grade bonds and non-investment grade bonds, and it is drawn just below Standard & Poor's BBB and Moody's Baa levels as shown opposite.

Standard & Poor's/Fitch Ratings	Moody's Ratings
AAA	Aaa
AA	Aa
A	A
BBB	Baa
BB	Ba
B	B
CCC	Caa
CC	Ca
C	C
D	

Investment grade

Non-invest-ment grade

Exercise 6 – Credit Ratings

Please complete the following table in relation to credit ratings:

Credit rating	Standard & Poor's/ Fitch Ratings, Moody's Ratings or all three?	Investment grade or non-investment grade?
Aaa		
AA		
Ba		
BBB		
B		

The answers to this exercise can be found in the appendix at the end of the chapter.

7. Bonds or Equities?

Learning Objective 5.1.7

Understand the benefits and risk of leverage in a company's financing structure

When a company raises finance it has two broad choices – to raise money by borrowing (in the forms of bonds or bank loans) or to raise money by selling more equity. To illustrate the impact of choosing one over the other, we will further develop the example of Crazy Jet.

Let's assume that Crazy Jet at the start of the period is worth $100 million. The company has a good profitable year, filling its aeroplanes with passengers on both its existing routes and a number of new routes, and at the end of the year it is worth $120 million. That's an increase of 20% over the year.

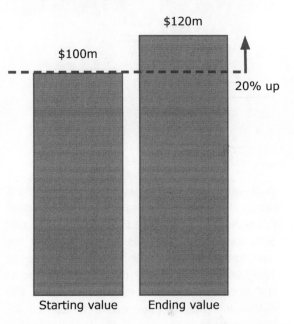

Starting value   Ending value

Now, if we assume that at the start of the period Crazy Jet was financed only by equity and had no borrowing at all, and no additional finance was raised during the period, then all of the 20% gain over the year will be to the shareholders. Their shares will be worth 20% more than they were worth before.

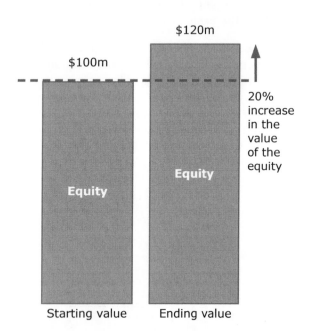

$120m

$100m

20% increase in the value of the equity

Equity

Equity

Starting value   Ending value

This means that the equity has grown from a starting value of $50 million to an ending value of $70 million. This is a 40% increase and will be preferred by the shareholders to the 20% increase they would earn if Crazy Jet were 100% equity-financed.

This is the beneficial impact of **leverage**. Leverage is the proportion of debt finance compared to equity finance in the company.

Exercise 7 – What if the Borrowing Had Been Even Bigger? Part 1

Try to assess the impact on the shareholders of Crazy Jet in the same situation, but this time with:

(a) 60% debt
(b) 90% debt

The answers to this exercise can be found in the appendix at the end of the chapter.

However, what if, instead of being 100% financed by equity at the start of the period, Crazy Jet had been 50% funded by equity and 50% funded by debt? Let us assume that the debt has not increased or decreased during the year; at the end of the period $50 million is still owed by Crazy Jet. However, all of the $20 million increase in value has been earned for the owners of the business, the shareholders.

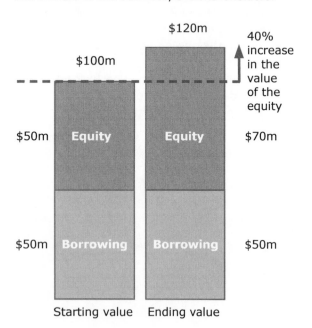

$120m

40% increase in the value of the equity

$100m

$50m   Equity   Equity $70m

$50m   Borrowing   Borrowing $50m

Starting value   Ending value

The impact of leverage is that, when a company like the fictional Crazy Jet performs well, it appears that the larger the proportion of the financing that comes from debt, the better. The larger the leverage, the more the gain to the shareholders is magnified.

However, two particular things have an impact on how much borrowing companies like Crazy Jet have:

* How much lenders are willing to lend, and how much they charge for that lending.
* The fact that, if the company does not perform well, a larger proportion of borrowing will have the opposite effect.

Expanding on the first point, providers of debt finance, like banks and bond investors, will consider the risks they face when making their loans. Simplistically, the more a company borrows, the greater the risks. As a result, the proportion of debt cannot go beyond the level that presents too large a risk for the lenders to be willing to lend. Furthermore, as the proportion of debt increases, the credit rating assessment will fall, which will make the borrowing more expensive, perhaps prohibitively so.

On the second point, if a company performs badly, then the impact of leverage magnifies the loss to the shareholders rather than the gain. Let's consider Crazy Jet again and this time presume the value of the business falls over a period, from a starting level of $100 million to an ending level of $90 million.

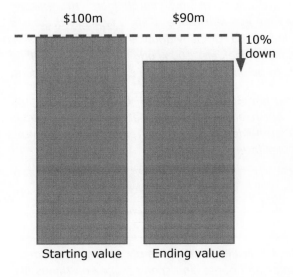

Clearly, if the business were 100% funded by equity, the shareholders would have suffered a 10% fall in the value of their investment. The shares were worth a combined $100 million, now they are only worth $90 million.

What would have happened to the value of their shares if the business had been 50% funded by debt and 50% funded by equity? Well, the leverage would have magnified the loss for the shareholders. The business would still owe $50 million in borrowing at the end of the period, so the equity would be worth the remaining $40 million. That is a 20% fall from the starting value of $50 million.

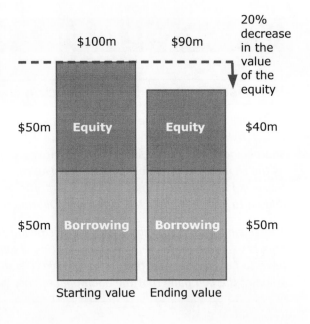

Exercise 8 – What if the Borrowing Had Been Even Bigger? Part 2

Try to assess the impact on the shareholders of Crazy Jet in the same loss situation, but this time with:

a.   60% debt
b.   90% debt

The answers to this exercise can be found in the appendix at the end of the chapter.

In summary, financial leverage is the proportion of a debt relative to the equity within a business. The greater the proportion of debt, the more gains in the business are magnified to the shareholders. However, the greater the proportion of debt, the more losses are magnified to the shareholders.

Exercise 9

The date at which a bond's life ends and the nominal value is paid by the issuer to the bondholder is known by all of the following, EXCEPT:

a.   Repayment date
b.   Maturity date
c.   Sale date
d.   Redemption date

⚙ Answers to Chapter Exercises

Exercise 1 – Crazy Jet's Financing

Crazy Jet might not have wanted to issue equity as an alternative to borrowing the money for two broad reasons. The first is that when more shares are issued to new shareholders, the existing shareholders' ownership stake in the company will become less substantial. This is typically described as the shareholders' influence becoming diluted. Simply put, if a company doubles its number of shares by selling new shares to new shareholders, the original shareholders' 100% original ownership will be diluted to just 50% after the new issue. Dilution tends to be unpopular with the existing shareholders.

The second is that raising finance by borrowing (debt) is potentially beneficial because of leverage. This is explored in detail in section 7 of this chapter, but relates to the fact that the borrowed funds have to be serviced and then repaid, while it is the shareholders who benefit from an increase in the value of the company that the additional finance has facilitated.

Exercise 2 – Government Bonds

The prime reason governments like the USA and the UK issue bonds is simply to fund their debt. Governments receive money mainly in the form of taxes and duties and spend money on things like benefits for the unemployed, medical facilities for the population and roads and railways. Just like individuals and businesses, governments need to find the money somewhere when they are spending more than they are receiving. Bond issues are typically used to finance the difference.

Exercise 3 – Yields

1. *$1,000 nominal value of a bond redeeming in 30 years is paying a 7% coupon and is currently priced at face value. The current yield on the bond is the same as the coupon rate at 7%. When the price of a bond is at nominal value, the yield is the same as the coupon rate.*

2. *If the above bond's price falls to $980, the yield will increase above 7%. The fall in price results in an increase to the percentage the investor receives each year. A purchaser will receive 7% of $1,000, having paid $980. This means the purchaser receives around 7.14% of their investment each year (based on 70/980 expressed as a percentage). If they hold on to the bond for the 30 years, the purchaser will also benefit from a windfall gain of a further $20 on redemption, having paid $980 and receiving back $1,000.*

3. *If the bond's price now increases to $1,100, the yield will decrease because an increase in a bond's price results in a fall in the bond's yield. For a buyer paying $1,100, the annual yield generated by the bond will fall to 6.36% each year (based on 70/1,100 expressed as a percentage) and the purchaser will also suffer a further loss at redemption when the bond will only pay back $1,000 after the purchaser paid $1,100 to buy the bond.*

Exercise 4 – What Happens to the Bond Price? Part 1

Situation	Price will go up, down, or stay the same?
The European Central Bank decreases interest rates in the eurozone. What is likely to happen to the bond prices of German and French government bonds?	**Up** When interest rates in general go down, bondholders are willing to accept a lower return when they buy bonds, so the price of the bonds will go up. This brings about a fall in yield.
The central bank in the UK (the Bank of England) increases interest rates. What will happen to the price of UK government bonds?	**Down** An increase in interest rates means that bond yields need to increase too, to keep them attractive to investors. The increase in bond yields is generated by the prices of those bonds falling.

In summary, interest rates and bond prices are said to have an inverse relationship – when interest rates in general rise, bond prices tend to fall, and vice versa.

Exercise 5 – What Happens to the Bond Price? Part 2

Situation	Price will go up, down, or stay the same?
Buddy inc is an oil exploration company and has just announced a significant discovery of easily accessible oil. What happens to the price of Buddy's 5% coupon-paying bonds?	**Up** The increased likelihood of Buddy being able to pay the coupons and repay the bonds should result in the yield required by investors falling and the price of the bonds rising.
Anemone plc's sales have suffered due to a recession in its main market. Anemone has a number of 7% coupon-paying bonds in issue – what is likely to happen to their price?	**Down** Anemone's credit risk has increased as its main market is in recession. The result is likely to be that Anemone's bonds will fall in price, resulting in an increase in the yield to reflect the additional credit risk.
Lakeground inc announces a substantial equity issue aimed at reducing its debt burden. What is likely to happen to the price of Lakeground's bonds?	**Up** A reduced amount of debt relative to the size of the issuing company will mean there is less risk that Lakeground may fail to pay the coupons and repay the debt. The lower credit risk should mean the bonds' prices increase, with the investors willing to accept a lower yield.

Exercise 6 – Credit Ratings

Credit rating	Standard & Poor's/Fitch Ratings, Moody's or all three?	Investment grade or non-investment grade?
Aaa	Moody's	Investment grade
AA	Standard & Poor's/Fitch	Investment grade
Ba	Moody's	Non-investment grade
BBB	Standard & Poor's/Fitch	Investment grade
B	All three	Non-investment grade

Exercise 7 – What if the Borrowing Had Been Even Bigger? Part 1

This is the impact on the shareholders of Crazy Jet if the value of the business had increased from $100 million to $120 million and it had been financed with:

a. 60% borrowing. The starting situation was that the borrowing was $60 million (60%) and the equity was $40 million. At the end of the period, Crazy Jet is worth $120 million. $60 million is still owed to the lenders and the balance of $60 million is the equity value. That is an increase of 50% from the starting point of $40 million.

b. 90% borrowing. The starting situation was that the borrowing was $90 million (90%) and the equity was $10 million. At the end of the period, Crazy Jet is worth $120 million. $90 million is still owed to the lenders and the balance of $30 million is the equity value. That is an increase of 200% from the starting point of $10 million!

Exercise 8 – What if the Borrowing Had Been Even Bigger? Part 2

The impact on the shareholders of Crazy Jet if the value of the business had decreased from $100 million to $90 million and it had been financed with:

a. 60% borrowing. The starting situation was that the borrowing was $60 million (60%) and the equity was $40 million. At the end of the period, Crazy Jet is worth $90 million. $60 million is still owed to the lenders and the balance of $30 million is the equity value. That is a decrease of 25% from the starting point of $40 million.

b. 90% borrowing. The starting situation was that the borrowing was $90 million (90%) and the equity was $10 million. At the end of the period, Crazy Jet is worth $90 million. $90 million is still owed to the lenders and the balance is an equity value of zero. So a 10% fall in the value of the business has wiped out the value of the equity completely!

Exercise 9 – End of a Bond's Life

9. C (chapter 5, section 4).

The end of a bond's life is alternatively known as the repayment, redemption or maturity date, when the bond's nominal value is paid to the bondholder.

6

Derivatives

This syllabus area will provide approximately 1 of the 30 examination questions

Derivatives

1. Introduction

Derivatives are not a new concept – they have been around for hundreds of years. Their origins can be traced back to agricultural markets, where farmers needed a mechanism to guard against price fluctuations caused by gluts of produce, and merchants wanted to guard against shortages that might arise from periods of drought.

So, in order to fix the price of agricultural produce in advance of harvest time, farmers and merchants would enter into forward contracts. These set the price at which a stated amount of a commodity would be delivered between a farmer and a merchant (termed the 'counterparties' to the trade) at a pre-specified future date.

These early derivative contracts introduced an element of certainty into commerce and gained immense popularity. Their popularity eventually led to the introduction of other derivatives, particularly futures and options contracts, and the opening of the world's first derivatives exchange in 1848, the Chicago Board of Trade (CBOT).

Modern derivatives markets have their roots in this trading of agricultural products and today's derivatives have widened beyond agricultural products to include financial instruments like shares and bonds, metals, energy and a wide range of other assets.

1.1 Uses of Derivatives

Learning Objective 6.1.1
Know the uses and application of derivatives

A derivative is a financial instrument whose price is based on the price of an underlying asset. The asset could be a financial instrument such as a bond or a share, or a commodity like oil, gold, silver, corn or wheat.

Derivatives come in a number of forms, including forwards, futures and options. Forwards have already been mentioned in the introduction to this chapter, and we will go on to consider futures and options in the following sections.

The way in which derivatives are used is fundamentally for one of two purposes – hedging and speculation.

Hedging

Hedging has already been touched upon in the introduction to this chapter. In essence, hedging involves replacing uncertainty with certainty so that risk is reduced. The farmer agreeing a price for his harvest in advance means he can plan with certainty and will not need to worry about how **market prices** might change between sowing seeds and harvest time. Similarly, the merchant has locked into a future purchase price and can begin to plan and prepare her price list for selling her agricultural produce with certainty about the mark-up she will earn. Both participants are using the derivative (the forward contract) to 'hedge' (reduce) the risks they face by replacing an uncertain price with a certain price.

Speculation

The second key use for derivatives is speculation, in other words using derivatives to make money. It is fairly obvious that someone might try to make money by correctly anticipating that the price of something, such as an agricultural product like wheat or barley, will increase. Without derivatives, the speculator could buy the wheat or barley, store it for a time while its price increases and then sell it at the higher

price to generate a profit. This would require the speculator to receive and store the wheat or barley, which will mean the speculator needs a temperature-controlled, weatherproof storage facility, such as a warehouse, and will also probably want to insure the grain in case of damage.

Speculating using derivatives could remove the need for storage and insurance completely – the speculator could use a derivative to commit to buy grain at an agreed future date at a pre-agreed price. If the price increases, the grain could then be sold onwards at a profit as soon as it is delivered, minimising the need to store and insure. In fact the speculator could choose to simply sell on the derivative, which will presumably reflect the increase in value, and generate a profit without even needing to take delivery of the grain!

But what if the speculator was not correct and the price of the grain fell in the period, instead of the hoped-for increase? Without derivatives, the speculator will have to sell their grain at a loss. With derivatives, the outcome is similar – the speculator will either both take delivery of the grain and then have to sell it at a loss, or alternatively choose to pay someone else to take on the derivative.

Derivatives also make it relatively easy to speculate on the price of something falling, rather than rising. If a speculator thought the price of wheat was going to fall in the near future, it is possible to commit to sell wheat now at the current market price. If the price falls, then the speculator can buy the cheaper grain and deliver it for the higher price agreed in the derivative. Again, the alternative would be to realise the profit by selling the derivative that enables the sale of something at a price higher than the market price.

Exercise 1 – Hedging Using Derivatives

A producer wants to hedge its revenues. Should the producer buy or sell forward contracts?

A consumer wants to hedge its costs. Should the consumer buy or sell forward contracts?

The answers can be found at the end of the chapter.

2. Futures

Learning Objective 6.1.2
Know the definition and function of a future

As mentioned in section 1, the CBOT opened the world's first derivatives exchange in 1848. The exchange soon developed a futures contract that enabled standardised qualities and quantities of grain to be traded for a fixed future price on a stated delivery date.

Unlike the forward contracts that preceded it, the futures contract could itself be traded. These futures contracts have subsequently been extended to a wide variety of underlying assets and are offered by an ever increasing number of derivatives exchanges.

A future is a legally binding agreement between a buyer and a seller. The buyer agrees to pay a pre-specified amount for the delivery of a particular pre-specified quantity of an asset at a pre-specified future date. The seller agrees to deliver the asset at the future date, in exchange for the pre-specified amount of money.

⚙ Example

A buyer might agree with a seller to pay US$60 per barrel for 1,000 barrels of crude oil in three months' time. The buyer might be an electricity-generating company wanting to fix the price it will have to pay for the oil to use in its oil-fired power stations, and the seller might be an oil company wanting to fix the sales price of some of its future oil production.

Futures contracts have two distinct features:

- They are exchange-traded – for example, on any one of a multitude of derivatives exchanges around the world such as the Chicago Mercantile Exchange (CME) or the London's ICE Futures exchange.
- They are dealt on standardised terms – the exchange specifies the quality of the underlying asset, the quantity underlying each contract, the future date and the delivery location. Only the price is open to negotiation. In the above example, the oil quality will be based on the oil field from which it originates (eg, Brent crude – from the Brent oilfield in the North Sea), the quantity is 1,000 barrels, the date is three months ahead and the location might be the port of Rotterdam in the Netherlands.

In the same way as forwards, futures can be used to hedge – replacing uncertainty about prices at a later date, with certainty about those prices. Futures can also be used for speculation – trying to make money by correctly anticipating a rise in price, or a fall in price.

Exercise 2 – Futures

An oil producer wants to hedge its revenues. Should it buy or sell futures contracts?

A speculator wants to make money out of an anticipated fall in the price of oil. Should the speculator buy or sell futures contracts?

The answers can be found at the end of the chapter.

3. Options

Learning Objective 6.1.3
Know the definition and function of an option

An option is a derivative that gives a buyer the right, but not the obligation, to buy or sell a specified quantity of an underlying asset at a pre-agreed exercise price, on or before a pre-specified future date or between two specified dates. The seller, in exchange for the payment of a premium, grants the option to the buyer.

There are two classes of options:

- A **call option** is when the buyer has the right to buy the asset at the exercise price, if they choose to. The seller is obliged to deliver if the buyer exercises the option.
- A **put option** is when the buyer has the right to sell the underlying asset at the exercise price. The seller of the put option is obliged to take delivery and pay the exercise price, if the buyer exercises the option.

The premium is the money paid by the buyer to the seller at the beginning of the options contract; it is not refundable.

The following example of an options contract is intended to assist understanding of the way in which option contracts might be used. It is an option that is based on a share – an equity option.

⚙ Example

Suppose shares in New Jersey inc are trading at US$3.24 and an investor buys a US$3.50 call for three months. The investor, Frank, has the right to buy New Jersey shares from the seller of the option (another investor – Steve) at US$3.50 if he chooses, at any stage over the next three months. If New Jersey shares are trading below US$3.50 three months later, Frank will abandon the option and it will expire worthless, and Steve will keep the premium Frank paid him.

If New Jersey shares rise to, say, US$6.00 Frank will contact Steve and either:

- *exercise the option (buy the shares at US$3.50 each and keep them, or sell them at US$6.00 per share), or*
- *persuade Steve to give him US$6.00 – US$3.50 = US$2.50 per share to settle the transaction.*

Assuming Frank paid a premium of 42 cents to Steve, what is Frank's maximum loss and what level does New Jersey inc have to reach for Frank to make a profit?

The most Frank can lose is 42 cents, the premium he has paid. If the New Jersey inc shares rise above US$3.50 + 42 cents, or US$3.92, then Frank makes a profit. If the shares rise to US$3.51 then Frank will exercise his right to buy – better to make a cent and cut his losses to 41 cents than lose the whole 42 cents. The most Steve can gain is the premium, ie, 42 cents. Steve's potential loss, however, is theoretically unlimited, unless he actually holds the underlying shares.

So, as seen, when a call option is purchased for speculative purposes, it is possible for the buyer to make a profit or incur a loss. In order to make a profit, the underlying asset on which the call option is based has to increase to a price above the exercise price plus the premium. The buyer of the option cannot lose more than the premium paid because the buyer has the choice of whether to exercise the option or not – if the exercise of the option is not worthwhile, the buyer will simply not exercise it.

It is also helpful to appreciate that in the real world, option contracts are typically for a minimum of 1,000 shares at a time. So the buyer of the call could gain or lose 1,000 times the amounts illustrated in the example.

To underline your understanding of call options in particular, please try the following exercise. The answer can be found at the end of the chapter.

Exercise 3 – Equity call options

ABC inc is a listed company and its shares are currently trading at $100 each.

In addition to the shares there are also equity options available on ABC inc shares. The three-month call option with an exercise price of $100 is currently available for a premium of $10.

Assuming you anticipate that ABC shares will increase in value over the next three months, please calculate the gain or loss the call option would produce in each of the following three outcomes:

Three months later, the ABC share price:

1. has increased by 20% to $120

2. remains at $100

3. has fallen by 5% to $95.

To complete the coverage of derivatives, below is a short exercise that tests and clarifies your understanding of the key differences between forward contracts, futures contracts and option contracts. The solution can be found at the end of the chapter.

Exercise 4 – Forwards, Futures and Options

1. Which one of the following derivatives gives the buyer a choice whether to go ahead with the contract or not?

a.   Forward contract

b.   Futures contract

c.   Option contract

2. Which of the following derivatives is/are traded in standardised sizes on derivatives exchanges?

a.   Forward contracts

b.   Futures contracts

c.   Options contracts

3. Which one of the following derivatives requires the buyer to pay a non-returnable premium?

a.   Forward contracts

b.   Futures contracts

c.   Options contracts

4. A speculator wants to have the choice as to whether to buy an underlying asset or not. Which one of the following derivatives is most appropriate?

a.   Buying futures contracts

b.   Buying call options

c.   Buying put options

5. A speculator wants to have the choice as to whether to sell an underlying asset or not. Which one of the following derivatives is most appropriate?

a.   Selling futures contracts

b.   Buying call options

c.   Buying put options

⚙ Answers to Chapter Exercises

Exercise 1 – Hedging Using Derivatives

A producer wants to hedge its revenues. Should the producer buy or sell forward contracts?

Producers (such as farmers growing agricultural produce or oil companies extracting oil) will hedge their revenues by selling their product at a pre-agreed certain price for delivery at a later date – selling forwards.

A consumer wants to hedge its costs. Should the consumer buy or sell forward contracts?

Consumers (such as cereal manufacturers needing agricultural produce or oil-fired power stations requiring oil for their furnaces) will hedge the costs they face by buying their product at a pre-agreed certain price for delivery at a later date – buying forwards.

Exercise 2 – Futures

An oil producer wants to hedge its revenues. Should it buy or sell futures contracts?

The oil producer will want to fix the price at which it can sell oil, so it will sell futures contracts. The precise number of contracts will depend upon the quantity of oil that is to be sold, and the standard size of each contract. For example, if the oil producer wants to fix the price for 10,000 barrels and the standard contract size is 1,000 barrels per contract, the oil producer will need to sell ten contracts.

A speculator wants to make money out of an anticipated fall in the price of oil. Should the speculator buy or sell futures contracts?

If the speculator is right, they will want to sell at the higher, current price when the price of oil has fallen to a lower level. So the speculator will want to sell futures contracts.

Exercise 3 – Equity Call Options

ABC inc is a listed company and its shares are currently trading at $100 each.

In addition to the shares there are also equity options available on ABC inc shares. The three-month call option with an exercise price of $100 is currently available for a premium of $10.

Assuming you anticipate that ABC shares will increase in value over the next three months, please calculate the gain or loss the call option would produce in each of the following three outcomes:

Three months later, the ABC share price:

1.   Has increased by 20% to $120

If the share price of ABC shares has increased to $120, the right to buy at $100 will be worth $20. However the buyer of the call option has paid a non-refundable premium of $10, so the net profit will be $20 less $10 = $10. The buyer of the call has essentially doubled their invested cash over the three months (generating $20, getting the $10 premium back and making a further $10).

2. Remains at $100

If the share price of ABC shares has remained at $100, the right to buy at $100 will be worth nothing since the shares can be purchased in the market for the same price. However, the buyer of the call option has paid a non-refundable premium of $10, so the net loss will be this $10 premium. The buyer of the call has lost the premium, which represents all of their invested cash.

3. Has fallen by 5% to $95

If the share price of ABC shares has fallen to $95, the right to buy at $100 will be worth nothing since the shares can be purchased in the market for the lower amount of $95. The buyer of the call option has paid a non-refundable premium of $10, so the total loss will be this $10 premium. Again, the buyer of the call has lost all of their invested cash, but thankfully cannot suffer a loss that is any greater than this.

Exercise 4 – Forwards, Futures and Options

1. Answer = c. It is only the option that gives the buyer a choice. If it is a call option, the choice is whether to buy at the exercise price or not. If it is a put option, the choice is whether to sell at the exercise price or not. Buyers of forwards and futures are both committed to buy.

2. Answer = b and c. Both futures and options are traded on exchanges on standardised terms. For example, a minimum commitment to buy or sell 1,000 barrels of oil, or perhaps the right to buy a minimum of 1,000 shares.

3. Answer = c. It is only options that require the buyer to pay a non-returnable premium. The premium is a payment made to have a choice – to exercise the option or not. Futures and forwards have no choice and, therefore, no premium.

4. Answer = b. Call options give the buyer the choice whether to buy or not. Put options give the buyer the choice whether to sell or not. Futures contracts give no choice, with the buyer committed to buy at the pre-specified price, on the specified future date.

5. Answer = c. Put options give the buyer the choice whether to sell or not. Call options give the buyer the choice whether to buy or not. Futures contracts give no choice, with the seller committed to sell at the pre-specified price, on the specified future date.

7

Markets

This syllabus area will provide approximately 4 of the 30 examination questions

Fundamentals of Financial Services

Markets

1. The Function of a Stock Exchange

Learning Objective 7.1.1
Know the function of a stock exchange

A stock exchange is simply a place where financial instruments can be purchased or sold.

It is where sellers are matched with buyers and transactions are agreed.

A stock exchange was originally, and still can be, a physical marketplace where interested buyers and sellers gather and enter into deals, commonly referred to as trades.

However, most exchanges have developed into electronic markets and only members of the exchange are able to access the electronic market.

⚙ Example

Roger holds shares in an international oil company that he is considering selling. He hopes to find other buyers and sellers of shares gathered at his nearest stock exchange and, find someone willing to pay a price that he considers reasonable for his oil company shares.

Roger would probably have to use the services of a member firm, such as a bank, to put his wish to sell the oil company shares onto the exchange's computer system. The exchange's system may have a number of interested parties that have already expressed a wish to buy the oil company's shares. As long as Roger is willing to sell at the same price a purchaser is willing to buy, the exchange's system will match Roger's order to buy with the appropriate order to sell. The exchange will then make arrangements to transfer ownership of the shares to the new owner and transfer the cash proceeds to Roger.

So, the function of a stock exchange is essentially straightforward. It is to facilitate trading in financial instruments, particularly shares – enabling sellers to sell their investments and enabling interested buyers to purchase investments.

Today, stock exchanges are found in most major centres such as New York, London, Frankfurt and Tokyo. A number of these have become major businesses themselves, arranging deals in millions of shares every day.

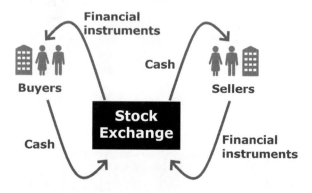

2. Initial Public Offerings (IPOs)

Learning Objective 7.1.2

Know the reasons why a company makes an initial public offering (IPO)

Stock exchanges do not arrange trades in the shares of just any company. Companies have to be accepted for trading on an exchange and become what is known as **listed** companies.

The requirements for companies to become listed vary around the world, but companies generally need to be well established and large enough to attract sufficient trading in their shares.

The process of a company becoming listed and having its shares admitted to trading on a stock exchange for the first time is referred to as an initial public offering (IPO). It is at this point that members of the public can choose to buy shares in the company for the first time.

You will recall that IPOs were defined in section 2 of chapter 4 on equities, where an IPO of the fictional CareerComic was considered.

⚙ Example

CareerComic is a business that provides a database of available careers portrayed in a fun, simple and understandable way – a comic strip of a day in the life of each career. It has been established for a number of years and the popularity of the product has made CareerComic very successful. It now has international appeal and, as well as being very successful in the US, it is being heavily used in Asia. The current shareholders decide that CareerComic needs to raise further money that will enable it to continue its geographical expansion, in particular the creation of a Mandarin version for the Chinese market.

CareerComic inc decides that it will offer new shares to the public in an IPO. Not only will the IPO enable CareerComic to raise money, but the publicity surrounding it will increase awareness of the product too.

The example of CareerComic highlights two of the typical reasons for companies becoming listed, or undertaking an IPO:

* raising money by selling shares, and
* increasing the public profile and awareness of the company.

The raising of money could be for the company itself, or it could be for some of the early investors deciding to cash in their shares or both. For example, the IPO of social networking site Facebook raised around $16 billion: $7 billion for the company and the other $9 billion for some earlier investors to sell some, or all, of their shares.

A further reason companies undertake an IPO is that it is much easier to buy or sell their shares after the IPO because the shares are then traded on a stock exchange. This is often described as the shares becoming more liquid.

CISI
CHARTERED INSTITUTE FOR
SECURITIES & INVESTMENT

3. Stock Exchange Indices

3.1 The Purpose of a Stock Exchange Index

Learning Objective 7.1.3
Know the purpose of a stock exchange index: single market; global markets

The larger stock exchanges, such as those in New York and London, trade millions of shares in thousands of companies every day. The prices at which those shares are traded change in response to a huge variety of factors, such as whether the company reports strong sales, whether a competing company launches a successful new product, and whether the unemployment rate decreases such that people have more money to spend.

The exchange will report the prices at which the shares are trading. This is clearly vital to the participants so that they can judge at what prices they may be able to buy or sell. There will also be a more formal report of the prices at which the shares are trading at the end of the day – the **closing prices**. As a result, it is easy to discover how well, or badly, a share's price has performed from day to day.

But how can investors get a feel for how well or badly shares are doing generally?

Thankfully, rather than having to amalgamate all the price movements, investors can just look at a stock exchange **index** instead. A stock exchange index, of which the most well-known is probably the **Dow Jones Industrial Average (DJIA)** drawn from New York share prices, performs the amalgamation for investors. If the index has increased, then prices in general have increased. If the index has decreased, then prices in general have decreased.

Such indices are sometimes drawn from the shares listed on just one stock exchange and are, therefore, referred to as single market indices. Others are drawn from shares listed on various exchanges internationally and are therefore referred to as global market indices.

One way in which a stock market index is used is shown in the following example:

⚙ Example

Stuart Radcliffe prides himself on selecting the best shares for his portfolio. He holds shares in ten companies that are all listed on the same market. His portfolio has increased by 12% on average over the last year. Stuart considers that his portfolio has done well.

However, it has been a good year on the stock market in general, and the index for the market has increased by 15%. So, the reality is that Stuart's portfolio has increased in value, but it has not done as well as the market average that is represented by the index – it has underperformed by 3% relative to the average portfolio.

Here the index is being used as a benchmark against which to compare the performance of a **portfolio** of investments.

The following section will provide some examples of the key stock indices around the world.

3.2 Example Stock Market Indices

Learning Objective 7.1.4
Know the following stock market indices and which market they relate to: Dow Jones Industrial Average; S&P 500; FTSE 100; DAX; Hang Seng; Nikkei 225

A stock market index is simply a number that amalgamates a group of share prices weighted by the size of the firm – so, the price movements of larger firms have a bigger effect on the overall index. As the shares in the group change value, the index also changes value but, in essence, if the group of shares goes up by 2% on average, the index will similarly go up by 2%.

⚙ Example

Here is the way in which index movements are typically reported in the press:

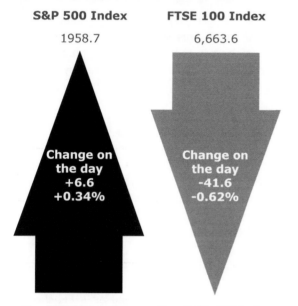

S&P 500 Index	FTSE 100 Index
1958.7	6,663.6
Change on the day +6.6 +0.34%	Change on the day -41.6 -0.62%

The S&P 500 Index was slightly up on the day, boosted by positive results from Apple

The FTSE 100 Index was slightly down on the day, after a negative assessment of Vodafone from Goldman Sachs

It is clear from the above that the significance of the index is how much it has moved, and that move could be largely attributable to particular shares that are included in the index. In the above examples it is Apple that has particularly impacted the S&P 500 Index and Vodafone that has particularly impacted the FTSE 100 Index.

The index value is termed points – as in 'the DJIA increased by 50 points today'. This means that the index went from perhaps 24,150 points to 24,200 points. The points have no specific value in themselves – the way to look at an index number is to compare it with a previous value, such as the previous day's number or the previous high.

Each index has a particular number of constituent companies. For example, there are 100 companies included in the **FTSE 100** and there are 500 companies included in the S&P 500.

Many stock market indices relate to particular markets, or geographies. For example, the DJIA consists of 30 large listed US companies that are listed either on the New York Stock Exchange (NYSE) or the NASDAQ. These indices are dynamic and the constituents regularly change. For example, one of the world's most valuable companies, Apple, has only been included within the DJIA's 30 constituent companies since March 2015 when it replaced AT&T.

The examination syllabus includes the requirement that candidates know which geographies five other indices relate to. All are commonly reported on the news, so you may already be aware of them. If so, the exercise below should be reasonably straightforward. If not, please feel free to look at the appendix for the answer and make sure you are clear as to which index relates to which geographical area.

Exercise 1 – Indices and Geographical Markets

There are six specific stock market indices that are listed in the table below and only the first one includes the geographical market that it represents. Below are the remaining five geographical markets in no particular order. Have a go at identifying which market relates to which index – the answers can be found in the appendix to this chapter.

Stock market index	Geographical market represented
Dow Jones Industrial Average	US
S&P 500	
FTSE 100	
DAX	
Hang Seng	
Nikkei 225	

Geographical markets
UK
US
Japan
Germany
Hong Kong/China

Now you know which geographic markets the various indices relate to, it should not be too difficult to work out which index (or indices) the following well-known companies are included within:

Exercise 2 – Indices and Companies

Which index (or indices) are the following 15 companies included within?

Company Name	Which index/indices? (DJIA, S&P 500, FTSE 100, DAX, Hang Seng, Nikkei 225)
Adidas	
Apple	
Barclays	
BP	
Canon	
Cathay Pacific Airways	
Coca-Cola	
Exxon Mobil	
Honda	
HSBC	
McDonald's	
Sharp	
Sony	
Toyota	
Volkswagen	

The answers can be found in the appendix at the end of this chapter.

Given that the stock market indices reflect the share prices of the constituent companies, it is useful to be aware of how the indices are doing – such as whether they are near the year's high or low. Please try the following assignment to enable you to get a feel for the current situation:

Mini-Assignment

Use the internet and/or newspapers to extract the current index and the last year's highs and lows for the following:

Index	Current level	High in the last year	Low in the last year
Dow Jones Industrial Average			
S&P 500			
FTSE 100			
DAX			
Hang Seng			
Nikkei 225			

An answer extracted in January 2019 is included in the appendix.

Exercise 3

What is normally used to ascertain whether share prices generally are moving up, down or sideways?

a.   Bank interest rates
b.   Stock market indices
c.   Bond yields
d.   Credit ratings

⚙ Answers to Chapter Exercises

Exercise 1 – Indices and Geographical Markets

The correctly completed table is as follows:

Stock market index	Geographical market represented
Dow Jones Industrial Average	US
S&P 500	US
FTSE 100	UK
DAX	Germany
Hang Seng	Hong Kong/China
Nikkei 225	Japan

Exercise 2 – Indices and Companies

Which index (or indices) are the following 15 companies are included within?

Company Name	Which index/indices? (DJIA, S&P500, FTSE100, DAX, Hang Seng, Nikkei 225)
Adidas	DAX
Apple	DJIA and S&P 500
Barclays	FTSE 100
BP	FTSE 100
Canon	Nikkei 225
Cathay Pacific Airways	Hang Seng
Coca-Cola	DJIA and S&P 500
Exxon Mobil	DJIA and S&P 500
Honda	Nikkei 225
HSBC	FTSE 100 and Hang Seng
McDonald's	DJIA and the S&P 500
Sharp	Nikkei 225
Sony	Nikkei 225
Toyota	Nikkei 225
Volkswagen	DAX

Mini-Assignment

Index levels as at January 2019:

Index	Current level	High in the last year	Low in the last year
Dow Jones Industrial Average	24,208	26,951	21,712
S&P 500	2,619	2,940	2,346
FTSE 100	6,862	7,903	6,536
DAX	10,931	13,596	10,279
Hang Seng	26,902	33,484	24,540
Nikkei 225	20,442	24,448	18,948

Exercise 3 – Stock Market Indices

3. B (chapter 7, section 3.1).

Stock market indices, such as the S&P 500 or the FTSE 100, give investors single figures that reflect the value of a number of shares (500 and 100 respectively for the S&P 500 and FTSE 100), giving a feel for how prices are generally moving.

Other Areas of Financial Services

This syllabus area will provide approximately 4 of the 30 examination questions

Fundamentals of Financial Services

Other Areas of Financial Services

Although the fundamental building blocks remain pretty much the same, the financial services sector is constantly evolving and it is vital for anyone working in, or aspiring to work in the sector to keep pace with these changes by scanning the news for important developments. At the time of writing there are some major political developments like Donald Trump's difficulties in implementing his election pledges after mid-term elections that resulted in the Democrats dominating the House of Representatives and the challenges in implementing the decision for the UK to leave the European Union ('Brexit'). In the US, Donald Trump may or may not get the funding for his 'wall' between the US and Mexico and any increased government spending will have an inevitable impact on US borrowing. Brexit might result in some financial services activities moving away from London and create more powerful financial centres in Europe such as

Paris and Frankfurt. Away from politics, there is the ongoing development of technology that is seeing more and more automation, particularly in the area of investment with so-called 'robo advisers'. Technology companies also continue to make inroads into areas of finance that were traditionally the preserve of the banks such as the growing importance of smartphone payments.

In this final chapter of this workbook, four areas will be explored in a little more detail – fund management; foreign exchange; insurance; and financial planning, particularly planning for retirement. Below is an introduction to each of the four:

- **Fund management** is where a firm creates an investment fund for its clients, which will enable those clients to invest together, sharing in any gains made or losses suffered. The investment decisions will be made by the fund management firm.

- **Foreign exchange** is the result of international trade or international travel – the money held by one party needs to be exchanged into another currency before a transaction can be completed.
- **Insurance** is a method of managing risk. For example, an individual may suffer from a serious illness that needs medical attention. An insurance company may be required to pay for the treatment under a health insurance policy.
- **Financial planning** is providing assistance to individuals, their families and businesses in organising their financial affairs to achieve their financial and lifestyle objectives. Within this, retirement planning is particularly important to individuals saving for the time of life when they will no longer be working. They will have to manage without earning a salary.

1. Fund Management

Learning Objective 8.1.1

Know the principle of collective investment schemes: comparison with direct investment; pooling; diversification; expertise

As stated in the introduction to this chapter, fund management is when a firm gives its clients the opportunity to invest in a fund which is an amalgamation of all of the clients' invested money. The fund's investments will be chosen by the firm, and the client investors will share in any gains or losses generated. This can be described as collective investment since the clients are investing together, and the fund can be termed a scheme – a **collective investment scheme (CIS)**.

The logic and features are best illustrated by looking at an example.

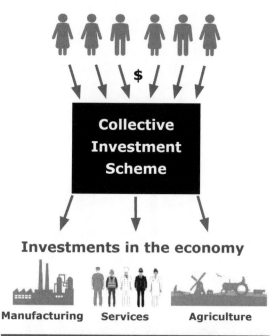

Investments in the economy

Manufacturing   Services   Agriculture

⚙ Example

Mohamed is a recent graduate with a good job. He is smart but knows little about investment, and he has been told it would be sensible to invest a modest amount of around $100 per month into equities, hopefully to enable him to afford a house one day. He particularly likes shares in technology companies as he feels technology is the future.

He could choose and then buy equities himself – termed direct investment. Why might that be a good or bad idea?

Looking at some of the more popular technology companies:

Assume Apple is trading at a price of $150 per share, Google is trading at $1080 per share, Microsoft® is trading at $105 per share and Facebook is trading at $147 per share.

With $100, Mohamed cannot afford to buy any of these shares. He would have to wait for two months before he has sufficient cash to buy a single share in Microsoft®, Facebook or Apple, and eleven months before he could buy a single share in Google – and that is assuming that these share prices do not go up in the intervening period.

This may be bad news on two fronts.

The first is that, he will have to wait before buying any one of these shares. But ideally he would like to put some money in all of these companies, because common sense tells Mohamed he is better off spreading his investment around. That way, if one of the shares does not perform too well, this will hopefully be compensated for by another of the shares doing well.

The second is that Mohamed is not really the person best placed to decide which of these technology companies is likely to do better. He is only considering these four companies because he has heard of them. There may be many more promising technology company shares available that he knows nothing about.

All of the difficulties highlighted in the example could be addressed if Mohamed were to invest in a fund rather than directly. Investing in a fund is described as indirect investment, because the investor invests in the fund, and then the fund invests in the shares.

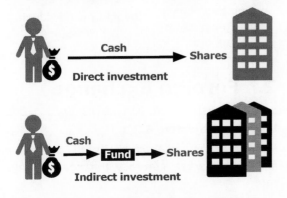

The first issue for Mohamed was that he had to wait two months to buy any shares because of the modest sums he was planning to invest, and even then could only buy into one of the three companies with shares cheap enough (Apple, Microsoft® or Facebook). This would have stopped him from benefiting from **diversification**. Diversification is simply the technical term for not putting all of your eggs in one basket – the more companies' shares held, the more likely it is that surprising bad news in one company is offset by surprising good news in another.

Diversification is a key advantage of a fund, because the fund is gathering together lots of individual investments and therefore is able to invest larger sums of money in a variety of different company shares. So if Mohamed were to invest his money in a technology fund, he would begin to solve his diversification issues.

It would only begin to solve the diversification issues because his portfolio could be further diversified by not confining his investments to just technology companies' shares, instead broadening his investments to include shares in companies in other sectors like pharmaceuticals, banks, industrials, oil and gas, media and food. After all, if a negative event occurs within a particular industry – for example, the technology sector generally suffering due to concerns about exploitation by terrorist organisations or poor defences against cyberattacks – it might be countered by positive events in other sectors, such as an increase in the price of oil.

Investing in a fund would also deal with Mohamed's problem that the money he has to invest is not large enough to buy a single share in companies such as Google and Apple. The size of the fund and the way it is structured enables investors like Mohamed to buy a portion of the fund for modest amounts of money, as shown overleaf.

⚙ Example

The Apple and Alphabet Fund

A fund manager has set up a fund to invest in the best-value technology companies, and advertises for investors. Each investor is only asked to invest $100. The fund manages to attract 1,000 investors – a total of $100,000.

The fund manager feels that the current best-value shares are those of Apple and Alphabet (the listed company that owns Google). He feels slightly more positive about Apple and uses the money to buy 443 Apple shares (costing $150 each) and 31 shares in Alphabet (costing $1,080 each). The remaining money in the fund is kept on deposit for the moment, ready to spend when the right opportunity arises.

The fund's investments are as follows:

Investment	Share price	Number of shares	Total
Apple	$150	443	$66,450
Alphabet	$1,080	31	$33,480
Cash	n/a	n/a	$70
			$100,000

Each investor's $100 is now invested in Apple and Alphabet, despite the fact that one individual Apple or Alphabet share is too expensive for $100 to purchase.

Assuming Mohamed uses his $100 to invest in this fund, he would now own 1/1,000th of the fund, which effectively means he has 44.3% of an Apple share and 3.1% of an Alphabet share, plus a little bit of cash.

	Share price	Number of shares	Total	M's I*
Apple	$150	443	$66,450	$66.45
Alphabet	$1,080	31	$33,480	$33.48
Cash	n/a	n/a	$70	$0.07
			$100,000	$100
* M's I = Mohamed's investment				

The fund has essentially allowed Mohamed and the other 999 investors to purchase a portion of an Apple and Google share.

The final issue that Mohamed faced was a lack of expertise. He knows little about the variety of technology companies that are available for investment and has difficulty assessing which technology companies are likely to do better than others.

Again this can be solved by investing in a fund. The technology funds that are made available by fund management firms are run by professionals who are constantly monitoring all of the technology companies and assessing which companies are the better investments. Each fund, of course, is likely to invest in considerably more than just two companies (Apple and Alphabet).

In summary, using a fund rather than directly investing will result in the following benefits:

- Money from a variety of investors is **pooled** into a single fund.
- This will enable the fund to benefit from diversification benefits that might not be available to individual direct investors.
- Fund investors are effectively able to buy **portions** of individual shares.
- The fund is run by a professional **fund manager**, who will be best placed to select the stronger investments.

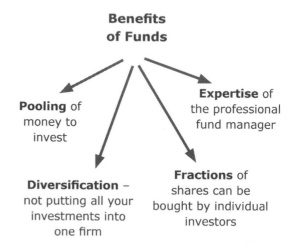

Benefits of Funds

Pooling of money to invest

Expertise of the professional fund manager

Diversification – not putting all your investments into one firm

Fractions of shares can be bought by individual investors

2. Foreign Exchange

Learning Objective 8.2.1

Know the basic characteristics of the foreign exchange market: currency trading; exchange rate

As introduced in chapter 2, foreign exchange (Forex, or FX) is an integral part of many business transactions and personal transactions when international travel is involved.

The smaller part of the **foreign exchange market** involves individuals travelling abroad, perhaps for holidays, as detailed in the following example:

⚙ **Example**

Usain is visiting London for a short break. He is normally based in the US, so all of his money is in US dollars. He knows he will need some

UK sterling to pay for taxis, buses, food and entertainment. He draws a lot of US dollars out of his US bank and sells them for UK sterling at the foreign exchange dealer's kiosk at the airport.

Usain has entered into a currency trade.

Exercise 1 – Usain's Transaction Part 1

The amount of UK sterling that Usain receives at the kiosk will be determined by the prevailing exchange rate between US dollars and UK sterling. The quoted rates might be as follows:

Quoted Rates

$s per £	1.25 – 1.35
£s per $	0.74 – 0.80

You can see there are actually two sets of quotes – the first is for the number of US dollars per pound; the second is for the number of UK pounds per dollar. Which of the two rates will be highlighted by the kiosk assistant for Usain?

The answer can be found in the appendix at the end of the chapter.

Each quote is also made up of two figures, a lower figure on the left and a higher figure on the right. The relevant side depends on whether the client at the kiosk is buying or selling the particular currency.

Exercise 2 – Usain's Transaction Part 2

Given that the following quote is the one highlighted by the assistant at the kiosk, how many pounds will Usain get, assuming he is selling $1,000?

Quoted Rates

£s per $	0.74 – 0.80

The answer can be found in the appendix at the end of the chapter.

How the two sides of a foreign exchange quote are applied is logical. The left-hand side is the number of UK pounds handed over for each US dollar, and the right-hand side is the number of UK pounds required for the kiosk to hand over a US dollar. Looking at the 0.74 to 0.80 rate, knowing that the quotes are the amounts in UK pounds per dollar, a US dollar will buy £0.74, and £0.80 is required to buy a single US dollar. If it were the other way round, clients of the kiosk could use a dollar to buy £0.80 and it would only require £0.74 to buy back the US dollar, leaving the client with a guaranteed profit of £0.06. That would be fantastic for the client, but the foreign currency kiosk is trying to make money, not lose it! The £0.06 is effectively the margin the kiosk makes.

Exercise 3 – Usain's Transaction Part 3

Usain's holiday break in the UK is now over and he still has £100 in cash. Assuming that the quote at the kiosk is still the same, how many US dollars can Usain expect?

Quoted Rates

£s per $	0.74 – 0.80

The answer can be found in the appendix at the end of this chapter.

Let's go back and investigate the relationship between the two sets of quotes that Usain encountered at the foreign exchange dealer's kiosk:

Quoted Rates

$s per £	1.25 – 1.35
£s per $	0.74 – 0.80

There is a mathematical relationship between these quotes. The left-hand side of the first quote represents the number of US dollars per UK pound. If this is 'flipped' by dividing it into 1, it reveals the following: $1/1.25 = 0.80$, the same number as appears on the right-hand side of the second quote.

The same is true when the right-hand side of the first quote is 'flipped' by dividing it into 1 ($1/1.35 = 0.74$). This gives the same number as on the left-hand side of the second quote. This is all logical. The number of US dollars a UK pound will buy ($1.25) should be based on the same rate as the number of UK pounds that are required to buy a dollar (1/1.25 = £0.80). Similarly, the number of US dollars that will buy a UK pound ($1.64) should be based on the same rate as the number of UK pounds that are received in exchange for a dollar (1/1.35 = £0.74).

Exercise 4 – Flipping an Exchange Rate Quote

A foreign exchange dealer is quoting the following rate for the number of euros per UK pound:

Quoted Rates
€s per £   1.245 – 1.255

Try to work out what the same quote would be, but expressed as the number of UK pounds per euro. The answer can be found in the appendix at the end of this chapter.

The more significant portion of the foreign exchange market is the result of transactions by companies, rather than individuals.

The foreign exchange market is huge, with the most recent survey of activity showing an average turnover of $5.1 trillion* each day! Within this total, the major currencies that are involved in transactions are the US dollar (around 44%), the euro (15%), the Japanese yen (11%) and the UK pound (6%)*. The most popularly traded pair of currencies is the US dollar and the euro with around 24% of the total.

The following example highlights how and why companies use the foreign exchange market.

⚙ Example

Pogo Gogo inc is a US company that manufactures and sells pogo sticks. With pogo sticks becoming increasingly popular with children, Pogo Gogo has just received a large order for pogo sticks from a large European retailer. It is the first order the company has ever received from outside the US, and the

European retailer is demanding that the price is agreed in euros and not US dollars.

When the money is received by Pogo Gogo it will be in euros, requiring Pogo Gogo to enter into a foreign currency transaction, selling the euros in exchange for US dollars.

Exercise 5 – Pogo Gogo Part 1

If Pogo Gogo sells €1 million worth of pogo sticks to the European retailer and the bank's quote for €/US dollar is 1.1394 – 1.1399, how many US dollars will Pogo Gogo receive?

The answer can be found in the appendix at the end of the chapter.

The foreign currency transaction that Pogo Gogo requires will be a currency trade that involves selling the euros it receives for US dollars. There is a danger that Pogo Gogo will not receive as many US dollars as it hoped for when the sale was agreed, because the exchange rate between the euro and the US dollar changes. However, the opposite could occur and Pogo Gogo may end up being in the position of receiving more US dollars than it had hoped for because the exchange rate has moved in its favour.

Exercise 6 – Pogo Gogo Part 2

The exchange rate at the time that Pogo Gogo made the sale was €/US dollar 1.1382 – 1.1387. When Pogo Gogo sold the €1 million worth, the bank's quote for €/US dollar was 1.1394 – 1.1399. Has the exchange rate movement worked in Pogo Gogo's favour or against it and what is the impact in US dollars?

The answer can be found in the appendix at the end of the chapter.

*Source: Bank for International Settlements (BIS) triennial survey 2016

These foreign currency trades are very common as a result of all the international business that takes place around the world. They are generally done with the banks – so in the above examples it would be Pogo Gogo's bank that will receive the euros and convert them into US dollars at the appropriate exchange rate at the date of receipt.

3. Insurance

Learning Objective 8.3.1

Know the types of insurance available: personal; corporate; the concept of syndication

The concept of insurance is straightforward – it is to put in place a safety net just in case something unfortunate happens. For example, most countries require individuals that are driving cars to be insured. So, if the driver is involved in a crash and is at fault, the insurance policy will be used to cover the cost of the crash, such as repairing the damage to the other car.

The insurance policy is provided by an insurance company in exchange for a payment, referred to as the insurance premium.

⚙ Example

Mack Radcliffe has just purchased a new car. He knows he needs to be insured and searches the internet for possible insurers. He finds that Draxa inc is offering insurance for a very competitive premium of just $80 each month. Mack takes up the policy and begins to enjoy driving his new car.

Mack is referred to as 'the insured', and he has entered into an insurance policy with Draxa inc as 'the insurer' or the 'insurance company'. The $80 monthly payment from Mack to Draxa is the insurance premium payable.

The above example relates to personal insurance because the insurance is being provided for an individual for their personal situation. There are many possible forms of personal insurance, such as insurance against the risk of theft from an individual's home (contents insurance) and insurance against the risk of sickness (medical insurance).

However, it is not only individuals that might find it helpful to use insurance as a safety net against unfortunate events. Imagine a small company that runs a general store – a fire or a flood could destroy most or all of the goods it holds for sale. Insurance taken out to cover the risks faced by companies rather than individuals is known as corporate insurance.

We saw in chapter 2 how insurance companies might reduce the risk they face by insuring large risks using reinsurance. Essentially reinsurance is an insurer taking out insurance against the possibility of a claim against the policy they have insured. Another possibility for the larger risks is that insurers each take a share of the risk using syndication.

⚙ Example

Total Shipping (TS) is a shipping company that has 100 container ships that move goods around the world. Each ship is worth around $100 million. TS is looking for insurance against the risk that any of these ships suffer damage through fire, adverse weather, mechanical fault or hijacking.

*Due to the size of the potential claim if something were to go wrong, it is tempting to think that the insurer for TS would need to be absolutely huge. However, the reality is that insurance will be provided by a group of insurers rather than just a single insurance company. This group of insurers forms a **syndicate** and each participant agrees to receive a set proportion of the insurance premium and bear an agreed proportion of any claim. If there were five participants that agreed to share the premium and the risk equally, they would each get 20% of the premium and bear 20% of any claim.*

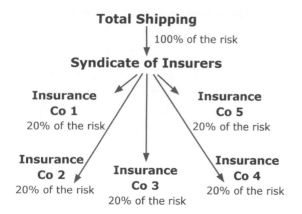

Total Shipping

100% of the risk

Syndicate of Insurers

Insurance Co 1
20% of the risk

Insurance Co 5
20% of the risk

Insurance Co 2
20% of the risk

Insurance Co 3
20% of the risk

Insurance Co 4
20% of the risk

As the above example makes clear, syndication is the grouping of insurers to enable them to underwrite substantial risks such as those of TS. The effect of syndication is to spread the risk around the insurance companies, which enables the insurance industry to take on insurance for even the largest, most expensive risks including damages caused by leaks from oil rigs or airline crashes and the like.

Exercise 7 – Types of Insurance

Here are four insurance policies that have been taken out. Please identify whether the insurance is corporate or personal.

Details of the insurance	Personal or corporate?
Shipping company Big Boats inc takes out a policy that will cover it against the risk of mechanical failure on its ships.	
Corporate executive James Yeats is concerned about his health and enters into a medical insurance policy that will enable any illness to be dealt with quickly in a private medical facility.	

Alistair McQuitty is a company director and has just been relocated by his employer to the Middle East. He buys a new car and takes out a local motor insurance policy.	
Exporta inc is an international business that exports mainly to countries in Africa. It takes out an insurance policy that will pay out if any of its overseas clients fail to pay for goods that have been shipped to them.	

The answer can be found in the appendix at the end of the chapter.

Insurance

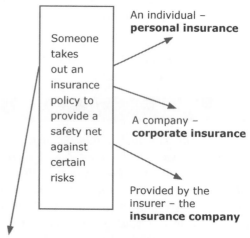

Someone takes out an insurance policy to provide a safety net against certain risks

An individual – **personal insurance**

A company – **corporate insurance**

Provided by the insurer – the **insurance company**

Where the policy is substantial, the 'someone' may be a **syndicate** of insurers, rather than a single insurer

4. Financial Planning

4.1 Introduction

Financial planning is a professional service available to individuals, their families and businesses, who need objective assistance in organising their financial affairs to achieve their financial and lifestyle objectives more easily.

Financial planning is clearly about financial matters, so it deals with money and assets that have monetary value. Invariably this will involve looking at the current value of clients' bank balances, any loans, investments and other assets. It is also about planning, ie, defining, quantifying and qualifying goals and objectives and then working out how those goals and objectives can be achieved. In order to do this, it is vital that a client's current financial status is known in detail.

Financial planning is ultimately about meeting a client's financial and lifestyle objectives, not the adviser's objectives. Any advice should be relevant to the goals and objectives agreed. Financial planning plays a significant role in helping individuals get the most out of their money. Careful planning can help individuals define their goals and objectives, and work out how these may be achieved in the future using available resources. Financial planning can look at all aspects of an individual's financial situation and may include tax planning, both during lifetime and on death, asset management, debt management, retirement planning and personal risk management – protecting income and capital in the event of illness and providing for dependants on death.

The CISI offers qualifications and related products at all levels for those working in, or looking for a career in financial planning. Further details can be found on the CISI's website.

A vital subset of financial planning is planning for an individual's retirement – retirement planning – and it is this that is specifically mentioned in the syllabus for this qualification.

4.2 Retirement Planning

Learning Objective 8.4.1
Know the importance of planning for retirement

As healthcare standards improve and medical advances continue, most of us will be lucky enough to live longer than our parents and grandparents. However, do we want and expect to continue working until we die? The answer to this for most of us is no.

Those of us expecting to enjoy a lengthy retirement must recognise that this will need to be funded in some way – the bills will still need to be paid and we will still need to put food on the table. Putting money away to use in retirement is called retirement planning.

The money earmarked for retirement is often termed a pension and there are three potential sources of pension, as shown overleaf.

Pension Sources

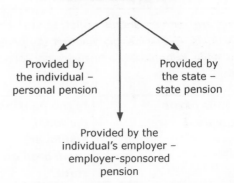

Provided by the individual – personal pension

Provided by the state – state pension

Provided by the individual's employer – employer-sponsored pension

As can be seen, the most obvious source of a **pension fund** to cover an individual's financial needs in retirement is to put money into a **personal pension scheme**. These schemes are typically made available by banks, insurance companies and fund managers. They generally involve the individual putting a proportion of their monthly salary into a pension scheme, which the pension scheme then invests in various shares, bonds and other financial assets. The expectation is that the contributions into the scheme, plus the potential growth in the value of the investments, will provide the individual with enough money to fund a relaxed retirement. Clearly the more money that is invested and the earlier it is invested (to maximise the potential for it to grow), the more comfortable retirement is likely to be.

It is also common for the firm that an individual works for to provide a pension scheme. This may attract good-quality staff as well as encourage them to stay. These employer pension schemes can be paid for completely by the firm (fully funded scheme) or might require the employee to contribute a proportion too (contributory scheme).

A number of countries around the world will provide a pension to their citizens in their retirement years, known as state schemes. However, these schemes are generally insufficient to fund what most of us would describe as a comfortable retirement. The state scheme will need to be supplemented if anything more than a very basic level of retirement income is expected.

Exercise 8 – Types of Pension

Here are some details relating to three individuals. Please identify whether the pension they have is personal, employer-sponsored or state.

Details of the individual	Is the pension personal, employer-sponsored or state?
Steven is employed by Dareds inc. Dareds have a pension scheme into which Steven pays some money that is supplemented by the company.	
Conrad is approaching retirement and has never contributed to any pension, nor worked for an employer providing a pension.	
Abdullah is self-employed and has a pension scheme that he has been contributing to for many years.	

The answer can be found in the appendix at the end of the chapter.

⚙ Example

Mr Average is a 48-year-old UK resident. He is employed, but his employer does not provide him with any pension and he has not set up a personal pension scheme. His children have grown up and left the family home and he is beginning to think about his retirement. His earnings are currently £509 per week.

Mr Average uses the internet to discover how much state pension he can expect when he retires. He is shocked to find that the maximum he can expect is less than a quarter of his earnings, at £119 per week. He is worried. Despite the fact that life may be cheaper in retirement as he will not have to travel to and from work and should have paid off his mortgage, he does not think he will be able to make ends meet. He immediately sets up a meeting with a financial adviser to discuss setting up a personal pension scheme.

The above example of Mr Average actually uses the UK's 2018 average level of earnings of £569 per week and the UK's maximum **state pension** of almost £130 per week (2019–20).

Mr Average will probably struggle to build up a substantial personal pension as he is starting so late in life. The longer pension money is invested for, the more opportunity it has to grow. He should have started his retirement planning earlier to fund the shortfall between the amount of money he will receive from his state pension in his retirement and the amount of income that will enable him to enjoy life.

As mentioned earlier, people are generally living longer due to medical, nutritional and social advances, and this increase in life expectancy has a serious impact on pension provision. This problem is typically referred to as the longevity issue – as people live longer, how will their need for a larger amount to provide them with a pension be financed?

⚙ Example

In the US, life expectancy has increased significantly in the recent past. World Bank data shows that those born in 1960 have a life expectancy of almost 70 years, and those born in 2015 have an increased life expectancy of almost 79 years.

US life expectancy

Year of birth	Life expectancy (years)
1960	69.8
1980	73.6
2000	76.6
2010	78.5
2015	78.7

This has ramifications for pensions. An individual born in 1960 and retiring at 65 years of age on average will only need a five-year pension, but this requirement increases to almost 14 years for individuals born in 2015.

As individuals live longer, the funding required for the same level of pension increases. If the pension is a personal pension, the solution is to pay more into the pension, work for more years and retire later or do both: combine greater contributions with a later retirement date. If it is an employer-sponsored pension the employer may be willing to pay more into the pension, but the impact this will have on the employer's profitability may mean that it needs to be combined with a later retirement date. For the state, a longer life simply means more money is required, which will mean higher taxes will need to be collected from the working population to pay for the pensioners who are living longer.

Mini-Assignment

Life expectancy in selected countries

Please use the internet to discover the current life expectancy in the following six countries.

Country	Life expectancy (years)
China	
India	
Japan	
Mozambique	
Sri Lanka	
UK	

An answer extracting details from 2019 is shown in the appendix to this chapter.

Exercise 9 – Mr Slater

Mr Slater is a 40-year-old UK resident and a self-employed writer. He has contributed to a personal pension for a number of years and continues to make monthly payments into his pension scheme. He is planning to retire at 60 and move to a cottage on the coast. He has recently read the good news that life expectancy has increased in the UK. On reflection, he starts to think about the impact this may have on his pension. What steps would you advise?

The answer to this exercise can be found in the appendix at the end of this chapter.

In summary, the importance of retirement planning is that, if an individual wants to enjoy a comfortable retirement, it is vital to put money into some form of pension scheme. Generally, it is sensible to start contributing to a pension earlier rather than later, to take advantage of the potential growth in the value of the investments made.

However, the reality for many people is that it is only after some years in work that earnings have increased sufficiently to enable them to save for a pension.

Exercise 10

For an individual with modest sums of money to invest in shares and a cautious attitude to risk, which of the following is likely to be most appropriate?

a.   Indirect investment
b.   Direct investment
c.   Buying the shares with the lowest prices
d.   Buying the shares with the highest prices

⚙ Answers to Chapter Exercises and Assignments

Exercise 1 – Usain's Transaction Part 1

The amount of UK sterling that Usain receives at the kiosk will be determined by the prevailing exchange rate between US dollars and UK sterling. The quoted rates might be as follows:

Quoted Rates

$s per £	*1.25 – 1.35*
£s per $	*0.74 – 0.80*

You can see there are actually two sets of quotes – the first is for the number of US dollars per pound, the second is for the number of UK pounds per dollar.

Which of the two rates will be highlighted by the kiosk assistant for Usain?

The relevant rate for Usain is the number of UK pounds per US dollar, since he is selling dollars for UK pounds, so the 0.74 – 0.80 is the quote that will be highlighted.

Exercise 2 – Usain's Transaction Part 2

Quoted Rates

£s per $	*0.74 – 0.80*

The left-hand side of the quote gives the amount of UK pounds that each dollar will buy, and is the relevant quote for Usain. The right-hand side is the amount of UK pounds that would be required to buy a single US dollar.

So Usain's $1,000 will buy £740 ($1,000 x 0.74).

Exercise 3 – Usain's Transaction Part 3

Usain's holiday break in the UK is now over and he still has £100 in cash. Assuming that the quote at the kiosk is as follows:

Quoted Rates

£s per $	*0.74 – 0.80*

Usain will be able to sell his £100 and buy dollars for £0.65 each. This will generate $125 (based on £100/0.80 = $125.00). You may remember the second quote from the kiosk. This quote would have enabled this question to be answered more easily – it gave the number of US dollars per pound.

Quoted Rates

$s per £	*1.25 – 1.35*

In Usain's situation his £100 would buy $1.25 each, which gives the same result of $125.

Exercise 4 – Flipping an Exchange Rate Quote

The foreign exchange dealer's quote of euros per UK pound needs to be flipped to provide the number of UK pounds per euro:

£s per €: 1/1.255 = 0.797 – 1/1.245 = 0.803

So the quote would be £s per €: 0.797 – 0.803

Exercise 5 – Pogo Gogo Part 1

Assuming that Pogo Gogo sells €1 million of pogo sticks to the European retailer and the bank's quote for €/US dollar is 1.1394 – 1.1399, Pogo Gogo will receive €1 million x 1.1394 = $1,139,400.

Exercise 6 – Pogo Gogo Part 2

The exchange rate at the time that Pogo Gogo made the sale was €/US dollar 1.1382 – 1.1387. When Pogo Gogo sold the €1 million the bank's quote for €/US dollar was 1.1394 – 1.1399.

Pogo Gogo received €1 million x 1.1394 = $1,139,400.

If the exchange rate had stayed the same, then Pogo Gogo would have received €1 million x 1.1382 = $1,138,200.

So the exchange rate has moved in Pogo Gogo's favour, and it has generated an extra $1,200 (the difference between the amount received of $1,139,400 and the amount based on the original rate of exchange of $1,138,200).

Exercise 7 – Types of Insurance

Here are the four insurance policies that have been taken out and the type of insurance – corporate or personal – plus a brief explanation:

Details of the insurance	Personal or corporate
Shipping company Big Boats inc takes out a policy that will cover it against the risk of mechanical failure on its ships.	**Corporate** Insurance taken out by a company is corporate and this policy may also have been syndicated as the risk may be too large for a single insurer to bear.
Corporate executive James Yeats is concerned about his health and enters into a medical insurance policy that will enable any illness to be dealt with quickly in a private medical facility.	**Personal** Despite James being a corporate executive, the policy is for James personally.
Alistair McQuitty is a company director and has just been relocated by his employer to the Middle East. He buys a new car and takes out a local motor insurance policy.	**Personal** Despite the fact that Alistair is a company director, the policy is for Alistair personally.

Exporta inc is an international business that exports mainly to countries in Africa. It takes out an insurance policy that will pay out if any of its overseas clients fail to pay for goods that have been shipped to them.	**Corporate** Insurance taken out by a company is corporate, and this policy relates to the risk that Exporta's clients may fail to pay.

Exercise 8 – Types of Pension

Here are the details relating to the three individuals plus the type of pension they hold and a brief explanation.

Details of the individual	Is the pension personal, employer-sponsored or state?
Steven is employed by Dareds inc. Dareds has a pension scheme into which Steven pays some money that is supplemented by the company.	**Employer-sponsored** Steven's pension was set up by his employer, so it is employer-sponsored, and since Steven pays some money into it as well as the company, it is contributory in nature.
Conrad is approaching retirement and has never contributed to any pension, nor worked for an employer providing a pension.	**State** With no other pension, Conrad will be relying on the state for any pension.
Abdullah is self-employed and has a pension scheme that he has been contributing to for many years.	**Personal** As a self-employed individual, Abdullah has sensibly contributed to a personal scheme.

Mini-Assignment

Life expectancy in selected countries (2019)

Country	Life expectancy (years)
China	76.6
India	69.1
Japan	84.1
Mozambique	59.5
Sri Lanka	75.7
UK	81.9

Source: World Population Review 2019

Exercise 9 – Mr Slater

There are two possible solutions for Mr Slater. He could choose to change his plans and retire later while paying the same amount into his pension each month. This would mean he works for more years, during which time he will pay more contributions into his pension.

Alternatively, he could keep his planned retirement date the same and put more of his earnings into his pension each month.

Clearly, he could also choose to combine putting more into his pension with a later date for retirement.

Exercise 10 - Indirect Investment

10. A (chapter 8, section 1).

Indirect investment in a professionally managed, diversified collective investment scheme is the most appropriate of the choices for the cautious individual with modest amounts to invest.

Glossary of Terms

ⓘ Glossary of Terms

Acquisition

A term used to describe the takeover or buying of a company by another.

Asset

Any item of economic or financial value owned by someone or a company.

Bank of England

The UK's central bank. Implements economic policy decided by the Treasury and determines interest rates.

Bankruptcy

The situation where an individual, company or other organisation is unable to pay its debts.

Bonds

Interest-bearing securities which entitle holders to annual interest and repayment at maturity. Commonly issued by both companies and governments.

Capital

Cash and assets used to generate income or make an investment.

Capital Gain

An increase in the market value of a security (ie, the value of the asset is greater than the price they were bought for).

Central Bank

Central banks typically have responsibility for setting a nation's or a region's short-term interest rate, controlling the money supply, acting as banker and lender of last resort to the banking system and managing the national debt.

Closing Price

The price of a security, such as a share or a bond, at the end of the day.

Collective Investment Scheme (CIS)

A fund run by a professional manager that enables investors to pool their money. The manager selects the investments and the investors share in any increase (or decrease) in their value.

Commission

Charges for acting as agent or broker.

Coupon

Amount of interest paid on a bond.

Credit Rating

An assessment of a bond issuer's ability to pay the interest and repay the capital on the bonds. The best rating is triple A.

Credit Risk

The likelihood of a borrower being unable to pay the interest or repay the debt.

Currency

Any form of money that circulates in an economy as an accepted means of exchange for goods and services.

DAX

German shares index, comprising the largest companies (30 shares).

Dealer

An individual or firm acting in order to buy or sell a security for its own account and risk.

Default

The situation where a borrower has failed to meet the requirements of their borrowing, for example by failing to pay the interest due.

Deposit

A deposit is a sum of money held at a financial institution on behalf of an account holder for safekeeping.

Diversification

Investment strategy of spreading risk by investing in a range of investments.

Dividend

Distribution of profits by a company.

Dividend Yield

Most recent dividend expressed as a percentage of current share price.

Dow Jones Industrial Average Index (DJIA)

Major share index in the USA, based on the prices of 30 major company shares.

Effective Annual Rate

The annualised compound rate of interest applied to a cash deposit or loan. Also known as the annual equivalent rate (AER).

Equity

Another name for shares or stock. It can also be used to refer to the amount by which the value of a house exceeds any mortgage or borrowings secured on it.

Exchange

Marketplace for trading investments.

Exchange Rate

Rate at which one currency can be exchanged for another.

Face Value

Also known as the par or nominal value. This is the amount that needs to be repaid on a bond. It is also the amount that is used to calculate the coupon payment (face value x coupon percentage = coupon payment).

Foreign Exchange Market

A market for the trading of foreign currencies.

FTSE 100 ('Footsie')

Main UK share index of 100 leading shares.

Fund

A collective investment scheme where money is combined and invested in a portfolio of shares with a common investment purpose.

Fund Manager

A firm that invests money on behalf of customers.

Index

A statistical measure of the changes in a selection of stocks representing a portion of the overall market.

Inflation

An increase in the general level of prices.

Initial Public Offering (IPO)

A new issue of ordinary shares, whether made by an offer for sale, an offer for subscription or a placing. Also known as a new issue.

Interest

The price paid for borrowing money. Generally, interest is expressed as a percentage rate over a period of time, such as 5% per annum.

Investment Bank

A business that specialises in raising debt and equity for companies.

Leverage

A measure of the extent to which a company finances itself from debt, relative to equity.

Liquidity

The ease with which an item can be traded on the market. Liquid markets are described as 'deep'.

Listing

Companies whose securities are listed on the LSE and available to be traded.

Loan

A form of debt where a borrower receives a certain amount of money from a lender. The borrower agrees to pay a contracted rate of interest to the lender and also agrees a date on which the loan will be repaid.

London Stock Exchange (LSE)

Main UK market for securities.

Market

All exchanges are markets – electronic or physical meeting places where assets are bought or sold.

Market Price

Price of a share as quoted on the exchange.

Maturity

Date when the capital on a bond is repaid.

Merger

The combining of two or more companies into one new entity.

Mortgage

A mortgage, or more precisely a mortgage loan, is a long-term loan used to finance the purchase of real estate (eg, a house). Under the mortgage agreement, the borrower agrees to make a series of payments back to the lender. The money lent by the bank (or building society) is secured against the value of the property. If the payments are not made by the borrower, the lender can take back the property.

NASDAQ

National Association of Securities Dealers Automated Quotations. US market specialising in the shares of technology companies.

National Debt

A government's total outstanding borrowing resulting from financing successive budget deficits, mainly through the issue of government-backed securities.

Nikkei 225

Main Japanese share index, composed of shares in the largest 225 companies listed on the Japanese stock exchange.

Nominal Value

The amount of a bond that will be repaid on maturity. Also known as face or par value.

Overdraft

A form of borrowing from a bank where the lending bank can demand repayment at any time.

Over-the-Counter (OTC)

Transactions that are undertaken away from an exchange.

Pawnbroker

A business that provides loans to individuals. The pawnbroker takes an item of security (such as jewellery) in exchange for the loan. The loan needs to be repaid for the borrower to reclaim the item.

Payday Loan

Very short-term loan that needs to be repaid on the borrower's next payday, usually the end of the month. Such loans are often very expensive.

Pension Fund

A fund set up by a company or government to invest the pension contributions of members and employees to be paid out at retirement age.

Personal Loan

A loan taken out by an individual where the precise purpose for which the money will be used is not detailed in the loan agreement.

Personal Pension Scheme

A retirement saving scheme set up by an individual, rather than set up by the individual's employer.

Portfolio

A selection of investments.

Premium

The regular payment made to an insurance company for insurance against a range of risks.

Redemption Date

The date at which a bond issuer has to repay the face value of the bond.

Reinsurance

The term for insurance taken out by an insurer on a policy that it has underwritten.

Retail Bank

Organisation that provides banking facilities to individuals and small/medium businesses.

Return

A measure of the financial reward on an investment, such as dividends and capital growth on a share. Return is always linked to risk: to have the possibility of a bigger reward, a bigger risk will need to be taken.

Secured

The situation where a lender (such as a bank or a pawnbroker) takes something of value. If the borrower fails to repay the debt, the lender is able to keep and sell the item.

Securities

Bonds and equities.

Security

A bank has taken security for its loan when it holds something of value. The most obvious example is if a bank takes security in the form of property ownership on a mortgage.

Shareholders

Those who own the shares of the company. Essentially, they are the owners of the company.

Start-Up

A business or company in its early stages. Typically start-ups are businesses that are not yet generating any profits.

State Pension Scheme

A retirement scheme that is provided by the state. Such schemes are generally not particularly generous and need to be supplemented by other forms of income in retirement (such as personal pension schemes, or pension schemes provided by the employer).

Syndicate

Insurance companies joining together to write insurance.

Trade

The purchase and sale of a security. Trades in shares are often agreed on exchanges.

Treasury

Government department ultimately responsible for the regulation of the financial services sector.

Unsecured

A loan provided to a borrower where the lender takes no security.

Multiple Choice Questions

Multiple Choice Questions

The assessment for this course will be a one-hour examination consisting of 30 multiple choice questions.

The following questions have been compiled to reflect as closely as possible the standard you will experience in your examination. Please note, however, they are not the CISI examination questions themselves.

Tick one answer for each question. When you have completed all questions, refer to the end of this section for the answers.

1. Which of the following investments is likely to be the most risky?

    A. Bonds issued by a start-up company
    B. Equities issued by a start-up company
    C. Equities issued by a large oil company
    D. Government bonds

2. A company paid dividends of 3.60 per share in each of the last four quarters. The share price is currently 198.50. What is the dividend yield?

    A. 0.02%
    B. 0.07%
    C. 1.81%
    D. 7.25%

3. If interest rates increase, what will normally be the effect on a 5% government bond?

    A. Price will rise
    B. Price will fall
    C. Coupon will rise
    D. Coupon will fall

4. Which of the following is one of the main benefits of indirect investment in an equity collective investment scheme managed by an experienced fund manager?

    A. Diversification
    B. Lower fees and charges
    C. Greater personal control over the investment decisions
    D. A fixed, guaranteed return

5. A company wishes to raise money for its overseas expansion plans, widen its public profile and increase the **liquidity** of its shares. Which of the following actions is likely to achieve all three things?

    A. Issuing international bonds
    B. Investing in a global marketing campaign
    C. Undertaking an IPO
    D. Seeking more international trades

6. If a credit card company quotes its interest rate as 20% pa, charged half-yearly, what is the effective annual rate?

    A. 20%
    B. 21%
    C. 22%
    D. 23%

7. In the event of a company going into liquidation, who would normally have the lowest priority for payment?

    A. Shareholders
    B. Banks
    C. The tax office
    D. Bondholders

8. A small company rents a shop located next door to a restaurant which recently had a major fire in the kitchens. It is worried about the cost of losing all its valuable stock if another fire were to spread further than before. What kind of insurance should it buy?

    A. Contents insurance
    B. Syndicated insurance
    C. Corporate insurance
    D. Reinsurance

9. Advising companies on M&A is one of the principal activities of:

    A. A corporate bank
    B. A central bank
    C. An investment bank
    D. A retail bank

10. How does a government typically raise money to fund its national debt?

    A. Issuing bonds to individuals and firms

    B. Making an appeal for donations from wealthy citizens

    C. Issuing equities on a stock exchange

    D. Doubling taxes for large corporations

11. An investor holds £1,000 nominal value of a 7% UK government bond trading at £97. What is the next gross interest payment that the investor can normally expect to receive?

    A. £28.00

    B. £33.95

    C. £35.00

    D. £36.05

12. When would the effective annual rate of a loan be higher than the quoted rate?

    A. When the borrower is unemployed rather than employed

    B. When the interest is charged monthly rather than annually

    C. When the loan is unsecured rather than secured

    D. When the loan is a bank overdraft rather than a personal loan

13. Which of the following has the right to vote at company meetings or assemblies?

    A. The holder of equities in the company

    B. The co-signatory of a contract of business with the company

    C. The largest clients of the company

    D. The holder of bonds issued by the company

14. You wish to invest money in some bonds. You wish to take as high a risk as possible in order to maximise your return. However, you do not want to buy bonds that are classified as 'non-investment grade'. According to the credit ratings given by major agencies Standard & Poor's and Fitch Ratings, which class of bonds should you buy?

    A. BB

    B. C

    C. B

    D. BBB

15.   The DAX is an index of which country?

   A.   England
   B.   US
   C.   Germany
   D.   Japan

16.   Which one of the following best describes what is meant by ethical conduct?

   A.   Complying with the law
   B.   Maximising the client's profit potential
   C.   Minimising the risk to the firm
   D.   Doing the right thing

17.   Banks provide one way of linking savers and borrowers. Which of the following best describes the way this link works?

   A.   Paying less interest on deposits than earned on loans
   B.   Paying more interest on deposits than earned on loans
   C.   Paying zero interest on deposits and lending the money for an upfront fee
   D.   Earning interest on deposits that is greater than the interest paid on loans

18.   Which of the following provides the opportunity for savers/investors to realise their equity investments?

   A.   Stock markets
   B.   Equity redemption
   C.   Government incentives
   D.   IPOs

19.   Outside of the US, the term 'commercial banking' is generally used to describe which of the following?

   A.   The way a bank makes money
   B.   A bank that specialises in providing banking services to businesses
   C.   A bank that only provides advice
   D.   A bank that specialises in providing loans and deposit facilities to individuals

20.   Which of the following is an example of a secured loan?

   A.   Mortgage
   B.   Overdraft
   C.   Credit card borrowing
   D.   Payday loan

21. Which of the following best describes an IPO?

    A. A company raising capital by selling equity or bonds

    B. A company generating its first profits

    C. A company raising money by selling shares to the public for the first time

    D. A company reaching levels of profit that are growing year on year

22. A shareholder typically has the right to all of the following, EXCEPT:

    A. Dividends from the company

    B. Vote at general meetings

    C. Sell their shares

    D. Regular coupons

23. When compared to equities, which of the following is considered an advantage to an investor in bonds?

    A. More scope for income growth

    B. Greater potential for capital gain

    C. Voting rights

    D. Regular and predictable income

24. Interest rates are suddenly and surprisingly increased by the central bank. What is most likely to happen to the price of fixed-coupon bonds?

    A. It will increase

    B. It will decrease

    C. It will remain the same

    D. The response depends on the credit rating of the issuer

25. Derivatives are used for two major purposes – hedging and which of the following?

    A. Speculation

    B. Risk reduction

    C. Insurance

    D. Reducing uncertainty

26. An investor buys an oil future. Which of the following best describes the investor's position?

    A. Obliged to deliver oil at a pre-agreed price on a future date

    B. Obliged to purchase oil at a pre-agreed price on a future date

    C. Obliged to deliver oil at a price to be agreed on a future date

    D. Obliged to purchase oil at a price to be agreed on a future date

27. Which of the following best describes the function of a stock exchange?

    A. To generate market indices
    B. To arrange the payment of dividends on shares
    C. To facilitate trading in financial instruments
    D. To provide a location for listed companies' general meetings

28. Which of the following indices is a narrow index that reflects share prices of US-listed companies?

    A. S&P 500
    B. Dow Jones Industrial Average
    C. DAX
    D. FTSE 100

29. The US $ per £ rate is quoted at 1.220 – 1.226. Which of the following is correct?

    A. $1.22 are required to buy £1
    B. £1.22 are required to buy $1
    C. $1.226 are required to buy £1
    D. £1.226 are required to buy $1

30. Mr Vance works at a company that provides him with a pension scheme that he does not need to pay any money into. How would the scheme best be described?

    A. Contributory
    B. Fully funded
    C. Personal
    D. State

Answers to Multiple Choice Questions

Q1.   **Answer: B**   **Ref: Chapter 2, Section 3**

It is generally the case that equities are more risky than bonds. It is also the case that when comparing two bonds, or two equities, the bonds or equities issued by the smaller, less financially secure entity are likely to be more risky than the bonds or equities issued by the larger, more financially secure entity.

Q2.   **Answer: D**   **Ref: Chapter 4, Section 3**

The dividend for the year is 3.60 x 4 = 14.40. The dividend yield is (14.40/198.50) x 100 = 7.25%.

Q3.   **Answer: B**   **Ref: Chapter 5, Section 4.1**

If interest rates generally increase after a bond issue, then to sell the bond the yield will have to increase to attract any buyer. The only way this can happen is by reducing the price. Therefore, bonds have an inverse relationship with interest rates: if interest rates rise, then bond prices will fall, and vice versa.

Q4.   **Answer: A**   **Ref: Chapter 8, Section 1**

Diversification is a key advantage of a fund, because the fund is gathering together lots of individual investments and therefore is able to invest in a variety of different company shares.

Q5.   **Answer: C**   **Ref: Chapter 7, Section 2**

The process of becoming listed, and a company's shares being admitted to trading on a stock exchange for the first time, is referred to as an initial public offering (IPO). Two of the main reasons for companies becoming listed, or undertaking an IPO, are raising money by selling shares, and increasing the public profile and awareness of the company. Another reason why companies undertake an IPO is that it is much easier to buy or sell their shares after the IPO because the shares are then traded on a stock exchange. This is often described as the shares becoming more liquid.

Q6.   **Answer: B**   **Ref: Chapter 3, Section 3.1**

20% divided by 2 = 10%, expressed as 0.10
1 + 0.10 = 1.10
1.10^2 = 1.10 x 1.10 = 1.21
1.21 − 1 = 0.21 x 100 = 21%

Q7.   **Answer: A**   **Ref: Chapter 4, Section 5**

If the company closes down, often described as the company being 'wound up', the equity holders are paid after everybody else. Equity is at the bottom of the 'food chain'.

Q8.   **Answer: C**   **Ref: Chapter 8, Section 3**

Insurance taken out to cover the risks faced by companies, rather than individuals, is known as corporate insurance.

Q9.   **Answer: C**   **Ref: Chapter 3, Section 6**

In addition to helping organisations raise capital, one major line of business for investment banks is mergers and acquisitions (M&A). This is where investment banks advise companies on their business strategy, in particular on how the companies can grow by buying other businesses.

Q10.   **Answer: A**   **Ref: Chapter 2, Section 2**

When government expenditure exceeds government revenue, the difference needs to be financed in some way and it is invariably borrowed. However, government borrowing tends not to come from banks but from individuals and firms in the form of regular issues of bonds.

Q11.   **Answer: C**   **Ref: Chapter 5, Section 3**

The interest is normally payable half-yearly and is based on the nominal value, ie, £1,000 x 7% x 6/12 = £35.00.

Q12.   **Answer: B**   **Ref: Chapter 3, Section 3**

If the frequency of charging interest is annually, the quoted rate and the effective annual rate are the same. When interest is charged more frequently than annually – for example quarterly, or monthly – the effective annual rate will be greater than the quoted rate.

Q13.   **Answer: A**   **Ref: Chapter 4, Section 4**

It is the equity holders that own companies. One of the key rights that owning shares provides is the right to attend and vote at company meetings.

Q14.   **Answer: D**   **Ref: Chapter 5, Section 6**

There is an important dividing line between bonds that are rated by the agencies as having less credit risk and therefore more appropriate for prudent investors and bonds that are more risky and therefore less appropriate for prudent investors. This is the dividing line between what are termed 'investment grade' bonds and 'non-investment grade' bonds, and it is drawn just below Standard & Poor's BBB.

Q15.   **Answer: C**   **Ref: Chapter 7, Section 3.2**

The DAX index is used in the German market.

Q16.   **Answer: D**   **Ref: Chapter 1, Section 1**

Ethical conduct often goes beyond what is laid down in the law and is perhaps best summarised by 'doing the right thing'.

Q17.   **Answer: A**   **Ref: Chapter 2, Section 1.1**

Banks pay less interest on deposited funds, than they earn on loans. The difference is used to fund the bank's operations and generate a profit.

Q18.   **Answer: A**   **Ref: Chapter 2, Section 4**

Facilities to sell equities are provided by stock markets, including world-famous exchanges like the LSE and the NYSE.

Q19.   **Answer: B**   **Ref: Chapter 3, Section 1**

In most parts of the world excluding the US, the term commercial banking is used to describe a bank that specialises in providing banking services to commercial entities, ie, businesses. In the US, it is used more broadly to cover banks that provide services to individuals and businesses.

Q20.   **Answer: A**   **Ref: Chapter 3, Section 4**

A mortgage is a loan made to facilitate the purchase of a home, with the property providing the security to the lender.

Q21.   **Answer: C**   **Ref: Chapter 4, Section 2**

An IPO is an initial public offer. It is the first time shares in a company are offered to members of the public and coincides with the company gaining a stock market listing.

Q22.   **Answer: D**   **Ref: Chapter 4, Sections 3 and 4**

Shareholders can get return from their shares by receiving dividends and selling their shares to generate a capital gain. As owners, shareholders can vote at general meetings. Coupons are paid on bonds, not shares.

Q23.   **Answer: D**   **Ref: Chapter 5, Section 5**

Unlike equities, bonds typically pay a regular, fixed coupon. However, they provide little in the way of potential for capital gain and no voting rights.

Q24.   **Answer: B**   **Ref: Chapter 5, Section 4**

Bonds have an inverse relationship with prevailing interest rates – when interest rates rise, bond prices fall and vice versa.

Q25.   **Answer: A**   **Ref: Chapter 6, Section 1**

Derivatives tend to be used for hedging or speculation. Hedging is using derivatives as a form of insurance, reducing risk and uncertainty.

Q26.   **Answer: B**   **Ref: Chapter 6, Section 2**

A future is an obligation in which the price is pre-agreed. Buying a future means the investor is committed to purchase the underlying asset (here oil) at an agreed future date.

Q27.   **Answer: C**   **Ref: Chapter 7, Section 1**

Stock markets are primarily trading venues for financial instruments, especially shares.

Q28.   **Answer: B**   **Ref: Chapter 7, Section 3.2**

Both the S&P 500 and the Dow Jones Industrial Average reflect US share prices. The DJIA has only 30 constituents, compared to the 500 in the S&P 500. The DAX is for German companies' share prices and the FTSE 100 is for UK-listed companies.

Q29.   **Answer: C**   **Ref: Chapter 8, Section 2**

The quote is the number of dollars per pound and the lower rate will be the number of dollars a single pound will buy. The higher rate will be the number of dollars needed to buy a single pound.

Q30.   **Answer: B**   **Ref: Chapter 8, Section 4.2**

Since Mr Vance is not required to contribute, the scheme is described as 'fully funded'.

Syllabus Learning Map

Syllabus Unit/ Element		Chapter/ Section
ELEMENT 1	**ETHICS AND INTEGRITY IN FINANCIAL SERVICES**	**Chapter 1**
1.1	**Introduction: Ethics and Integrity in Financial Services** On completion, the candidate should:	
1.1.1	Know the key principles of ethical behaviour in financial services	Section 1
ELEMENT 2	**SAVING AND BORROWING**	**Chapter 2**
2.2	**Savers/Borrowers** On completion, the candidate should:	
2.1.1	Know how the financial services sector can be viewed as linking those with surplus money (savers) and those with a need for money (borrowers) in the following ways: • via banks (deposits, loans) • via equities (ownership stake) • via bonds (IOUs)	Section 1
2.1.2	Know that borrowers include companies and governments and that governments issue bonds rather than equities	Section 2
2.1.3	Know the relationship between the level of risk and the prospect of reward	Section 3
2.1.4	Know that the financial services sector also includes markets to enable investors in equities and bonds to buy or sell investments	Section 4
2.1.5	Know that the financial services sector also includes insurance providers to enable financial risks to be managed	Section 5
2.1.6	Know that the financial services sector also includes foreign exchange dealers to allow one currency to be exchanged for another to facilitate international trade	Section 6
ELEMENT 3	**BANKING**	**Chapter 3**
3.1	**Banking** On completion, the candidate should:	
3.1.1	Know the difference between retail and commercial banking and the types of customer – individuals/corporates	Section 1
3.1.2	Know the nature and types of borrowing available to retail customers: • from banks – loans, mortgage loans, overdrafts • from banks and credit card companies – credit cards • from other sources – pawnbrokers, payday loans	Section 2
3.1.3	Know the difference between the quoted interest rate on borrowing and the effective annual rate of borrowing	Section 3
3.1.4	Be able to calculate the effective annual rate given the quoted rate and frequency of interest payment	Section 3.1
3.1.5	Know the difference between secured and unsecured borrowing	Section 4
3.1.6	Know what types of borrowing are likely to be relatively expensive – pawnbrokers/payday loans, credit cards, overdrafts, unsecured loans and cheaper – secured loans, eg, mortgages	Section 5

Syllabus Unit/ Element		Chapter/ Section
3.1.7	Know that investment banks help companies to raise money and advise them on strategy, eg, mergers and acquisitions	Section 6
3.1.8	Know the role of central banks: • banker to banking system • banker for the government • regulatory role (interest rate setting)	Section 7
ELEMENT 4	**EQUITIES**	**Chapter 4**
4.1	**Equities** On completion, the candidate should:	
4.1.1	Know the reasons for issuing shares (stock) – to finance a company	Section 1
4.1.2	Know the definition of an initial public offering (IPO)	Section 2
4.1.3	Know the potential sources of return from shares: • dividend • capital gain	Section 3
4.1.4	Be able to calculate the dividend yield given the share price and the dividends paid in the year	Section 3
4.1.5	Know that shares provide their owners with the right to vote at company meetings/assemblies	Section 4
4.1.6	Know the risks involved in owning shares: • lack of profit • bankruptcy/collapse	Section 5
ELEMENT 5	**BONDS**	**Chapter 5**
5.1	**Introduction to Bonds** On completion, the candidate should:	
5.1.1	Know the definition of a bond and the reasons for issue: • alternative to loans or issuing shares	Section 1
5.1.2	Know the bond issuers: • governments • corporates	Section 2
5.1.3	Know the features of bonds: • repayment date • frequency of interest payments • tradeable	Section 3
5.1.4	Know the key terms: • nominal • coupon • redemption/maturity • yield	Section 4
5.1.5	Know the advantages and disadvantages of investing in bonds: • regular income • fixed maturity date • credit risk	Section 5
5.1.6	Know the role of credit rating agencies: • investment grade/non-investment grade	Section 6
5.1.7	Understand the benefits and risk of leverage in a company's financing structure	Section 7

Syllabus Unit/ Element		Chapter/ Section
ELEMENT 6	**DERIVATIVES**	**Chapter 6**
6.1	**Derivatives** On completion, the candidate should:	
6.1.1	Know the uses and applications of derivatives	Section 1.1
6.1.2	Know the definition and function of a future	Section 2
6.1.3	Know the definition and function of an option	Section 3
ELEMENT 7	**MARKETS**	**Chapter 6**
7.1	**Markets** On completion, the candidate should:	
7.1.1	Know the function of a stock exchange	Section 1
7.1.2	know the reasons why a company makes an initial public offering (IPO)	Section 2
7.1.3	Know the purpose of a stock exchange index: • single market • global markets	Section 3.1
7.1.4	Know the following stock market indices and which market they relate to: • Dow Jones Industrial Average • S&P 500 • FTSE 100 • DAX • Hang Seng • Nikkei 225	Section 3.2
ELEMENT 8	**OTHER AREAS OF FINANCIAL SERVICES**	**Chapter 7**
8.1	**Fund Management** On completion, the candidate should:	
8.1.1	Know the principle of collective investment schemes: • comparison with direct investment • pooling • diversification • expertise	Section 1
8.2	**Foreign Exchange** On completion, the candidate should:	
8.2.1	Know the basic characteristics of the foreign exchange market: • currency trading • exchange rate	Section 2
8.3	**Insurance** On completion, the candidate should:	
8.3.1	Know the types of insurance available: • personal • corporate • the concept of syndication	Section 3
8.4	**Retirement Planning** On completion, the candidate should:	
8.4.1	Know the importance of planning for retirement	Section 4.2

Examination Specification

Each examination paper is constructed from a specification that determines the weightings that will be given to each element. The specification is given below.

It is important to note that the numbers quoted may vary slightly from examination to examination as there is some flexibility to ensure that each examination has a consistent level of difficulty.

Element Number	Element	Questions
1	Ethics and Integrity in Financial Services	1
2	Saving and Borrowing	4
3	Banking	5
4	Equities	5
5	Bonds	6
6	Derivatives	1
7	Markets	4
8	Other Areas of Financial Services	4
Total		**30**

CISI Associate (ACSI) Membership can work for you...

Studying for a CISI qualification is hard work and we're sure you're putting in plenty of hours, but don't lose sight of your goal!

This is just the first step in your career; there is much more to achieve!

The securities and investments sector attracts ambitious and driven individuals. You're probably one yourself and that's great, but on the other hand you're almost certainly surrounded by lots of other people with similar ambitions.

So how can you stay one step ahead during these uncertain times?

Entry Criteria:

Pass in either:

- Investment Operations Certificate (IOC), IFQ, ICWIM, Capital Markets in, eg, Securities, Derivatives, Advanced Certificates; or
- one CISI Diploma/Masters in Wealth Management paper

Joining Fee: £25 or free if applying via prefilled application form   **Annual Subscription (pro rata):** £125

Using your new CISI qualification* to become an Associate (ACSI) member of the Chartered Institute for Securities & Investment could well be the next important career move you make this year, and help you maintain your competence.

Join our global network of over 40,000 financial services professionals and start enjoying both the professional and personal benefits that CISI membership offers. Once you become a member you can use the prestigious ACSI designation after your name and even work towards becoming personally chartered.

* ie, Investment Operations Certificate (IOC), IFQ, ICWIM, Capital Markets

Benefits in Summary...

- Use of the CISI CPD Scheme
- Unlimited free CPD seminars, webcasts, podcasts and online training tools
- Highly recognised designatory letters
- Unlimited free attendance at CISI Professional Forums
- CISI publications including *The Review* and *Change – The Regulatory Update*
- 20% discount on all CISI conferences and training courses
- Invitation to the CISI Annual Lecture
- Select benefits – our exclusive personal benefits portfolio

The ACSI designation will provide you with access to a range of member benefits, including Professional Refresher where there are currently over 100 modules available on subjects including Anti-Money Laundering, Information Security & Data Protection, Integrity & Ethics, and the UK Bribery Act. CISI TV is also available to members, allowing you to catch up on the latest CISI events, whilst earning valuable CPD.

Plus many other networking opportunities which could be invaluable for your career.

Revision Express

You've bought the workbook... now test your knowledge before your exam.

Revision Express is an engaging online study tool to be used in conjunction with most CISI workbooks.

Key Features of Revision Express:
- Questions throughout to reaffirm understanding of the subject
- Special end-of-module practice exam to reflect as closely as possible the standard you will experience in your exam (please note, however, they are not the CISI exam questions themselves)
- Extensive glossary of terms
- Allows you to study whenever you like, and on any device

IMPORTANT: The questions contained in Revision Express products are designed as aids to revision, and should not be seen in any way as mock exams.

Price per Revision Express module: £35
Price when purchased with the corresponding CISI workbook: £108 (normal price: £119)

To purchase Revision Express:

call our Customer Support Centre on:
+44 20 7645 0777

or visit the CISI's online bookshop at:
cisi.org/bookshop

For more information on our elearning products, contact our Customer Support Centre on +44 20 7645 0777, or visit our website at cisi.org/elearning

Professional Refresher

Self-testing elearning modules to refresh your knowledge, meet regulatory and firm requirements, and earn CPD.

Professional Refresher is a training solution to help you remain up-to-date with industry developments, maintain regulatory compliance and demonstrate continuing learning.

This popular online learning tool allows self-administered refresher testing on a variety of topics, including the latest regulatory changes.

There are over 120 modules available which address UK and international issues. Modules are reviewed by practitioners frequently and new ones are added to the suite on a regular basis.

Benefits to firms:
- Learning and testing can form part of business T&C programme
- Learning and testing kept up-to-date and accurate by the CISI
- Relevant and useful – devised by industry practitioners
- Access to individual results available as part of management overview facility, 'Super User'
- Records of staff training can be produced for internal use and external audits
- Cost-effective – no additional charge for CISI members
- Available for non-members to purchase

Benefits to individuals:
- Comprehensive selection of topics across sectors
- Modules are regularly refreshed and updated by industry experts
- New modules added regularly
- Free for members
- Successfully passed modules are recorded in your CPD log as active learning
- Counts as structured learning for RDR purposes
- On completion of a module, a certificate can be printed out for your own records

The full suite of Professional Refresher modules is free to CISI members, or £250 for non-members. Modules are also available individually. To view a full list of Professional Refresher modules visit:

cisi.org/refresher

If you or your firm would like to find out more, contact our Client Relationship Management team:

+ 44 20 7645 0670
crm@cisi.org

For more information on our elearning products, contact our Customer Support Centre on +44 20 7645 0777, or visit our website at cisi.org/refresher

Professional Refresher

Top 5

SCORM COMPLIANT

Integrity & Ethics
- High-Level View
- Ethical Behaviour
- An Ethical Approach
- Compliance vs Ethics

Anti-Money Laundering
- Introduction to Money Laundering
- UK Legislation and Regulation
- Money Laundering Regulations 2017
- Proceeds of Crime Act 2002
- Terrorist Financing
- Suspicious Activity Reporting
- Money Laundering Reporting Officer
- Sanctions

General Data Protection Regulation (GDPR)
- Understanding the Terminology
- The Six Data Protection Principles
- Data Subject Rights
- Technical and Organisational Measures

Information Security and Data Protection
- Cyber-Security
- The Regulators

UK Bribery Act
- Background to the Act
- The Offences
- What the Offences Cover
- When Has an Offence Been Committed?
- The Defences Against Charges of Bribery
- The Penalties

Latest

Cryptocurrencies
- Bitcoin
- Altcoins
- Central Bank Digital Currency and Cryptofiat
- Trading Cryptocurrencies
- The Impact of Cryptocurrencies

Change Management
- Types of Change
- Change Theories
- The Complexities of Change
- Leading Change
- Key Skills and Competencies

Regulatory Update
- General Regulatory Changes
- Sector Changes

Common Reporting Standard (CRS)
- What is the CRS?
- Implementation and Compliance
- Practical Issues
- The Global Perspective

Cross-Border Investment Services
- The UK System
- Overseas Regulation
- Applicability
- Face-to-Face Meetings
- Distance Communications
- Brexit Implications
- Gifts and Entertainment
- Tax Evasion, Money Laundering, and Terrorist Financing

Operations

Best Execution
- What Is Best Execution?
- Achieving Best Execution
- Order Execution Policies
- Information to Clients & Client Consent
- Monitoring, the Rules, and Instructions
- Best Execution for Specific Types of Firms

Approved Persons Regime
- The Basis of the Regime
- Fitness and Propriety
- The Controlled Functions
- Principles for Approved Persons
- The Code of Practice for Approved Persons

Corporate Actions
- Corporate Structure and Finance
- Life Cycle of an Event
- Mandatory Events
- Voluntary Events

Wealth

Client Assets and Client Money
- Protecting Client Assets and Client Money
- Segregation and Holding
- Due Diligence of Custodians and Banks
- Reconciliations
- Records and Accounts
- CASS Oversight

Investment Principles and Risk
- Diversification
- Factfind and Risk Profiling
- Investment Management
- Modern Portfolio Theory and Investing Styles
- Direct and Indirect Investments
- Socially Responsible Investment
- Collective Investments
- Investment Trusts
- Dealing in Debt Securities and Equities

Banking Standards
- Introduction and Background
- Strengthening Individual Accountability
- Reforming Corporate Governance
- Securing Better Outcomes for Consumers
- Enhancing Financial Stability

Suitability of Client Investments
- Assessing Suitability
- Risk Profiling
- Establishing Risk Appetite
- Obtaining Customer Information
- Suitable Questions and Answers
- Making Suitable Investment Selections
- Guidance, Reports and Record Keeping

International

Foreign Account Tax Compliance Act (FATCA)
- Foreign Financial Institutions
- Due Diligence Requirements
- Reporting
- Compliance

MiFID II
- The Organisations Covered by MiFID II
- The Products Subject to MiFID II
- The Origins of MiFID II
- The Impact of MiFID II
- The Products Covered by MiFID II
- Cross-Border Business Under MiFID II

UCITS
- The Original UCITS Directive
- UCITS III
- UCITS IV
- Non-UCITS Funds
- Latest Developments

cisi.org/refresher

Feedback to the CISI

Have you found this workbook to be a valuable aid to your studies? We would like your views, so please email us at learningresources@cisi.org with any thoughts, ideas or comments.

Accredited Training Partners

Support for exam students studying for the Chartered Institute for Securities & Investment (CISI) qualifications is provided by several Accredited Training Partners (ATPs), including Fitch Learning and BPP. The CISI's ATPs offer a range of face-to-face training courses, distance learning programmes, their own learning resources and study packs which have been accredited by the CISI. The CISI works in close collaboration with its ATPs to ensure they are kept informed of changes to CISI exams so they can build them into their own courses and study packs.

CISI Workbook Specialists Wanted

Workbook Authors

Experienced freelance authors with finance experience, and who have published work in their area of specialism, are sought. Responsibilities include:

- Updating workbooks in line with new syllabuses and any industry developments
- Ensuring that the syllabus is fully covered

Workbook Reviewers

Individuals with a high-level knowledge of the subject area are sought. Responsibilities include:

- Highlighting any inconsistencies against the syllabus
- Assessing the author's interpretation of the workbook

Workbook Technical Reviewers

Technical reviewers to provide a detailed review of the workbook and bring the review comments to the panel. Responsibilities include:

- Cross-checking the workbook against the syllabus
- Ensuring sufficient coverage of each learning objective

Workbook Proofreaders

Proofreaders are needed to proof workbooks both grammatically and also in terms of the format and layout. Responsibilities include:

- Checking for spelling and grammar mistakes
- Checking for formatting inconsistencies

If you are interested in becoming a CISI external specialist call:
+44 20 7645 0609

or email:
externalspecialists@cisi.org

For bookings, orders, membership and general enquiries please contact our Customer Support Centre on +44 20 7645 0777, or visit our website at cisi.org